A]
An Egyptian Meets His Neighbors

Ali Salem

The Moshe Dayan Center for Middle Eastern and African Studies seeks to contribute by research, documentation, and publication to the study and understanding of the modern history and current affairs of the Middle East and Africa. The Center is part of the School of History and the Lester and Sally Entin Faculty of Humanities at Tel Aviv University.

The Dayan Center Papers are monographs, collections of articles, and conference proceedings resulting from research done by the Center's fellows, associates, and guests. The series is a continuation of the Center's *Occasional Papers* series, published since 1970, and is edited by Ami Ayalon, a senior research associate at the Moshe Dayan Center.

The Dayan Center Papers are published by the Moshe Dayan Center and distributed worldwide by Syracuse University Press, 1600 Jamesville Avenue, Syracuse, NY 13244–5160; and in Israel by the Publications Department, the Moshe Dayan Center for Middle Eastern and African Studies, Tel Aviv University, Ramat Aviv 69978.

A Drive to Israel

An Egyptian Meets His Neighbors

Ali Salem

Translated from the Arabic
by Robert J. Silverman

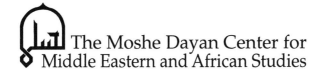 The Moshe Dayan Center for
Middle Eastern and African Studies

Tel Aviv University

To a person whom I will not meet
again on a new trip to Israel,
since he has departed this world
leaving behind an immortal legacy.

Tawfiq Ziyad
poet, statesman and human being

Contents

Translator's Note

Ali Salem announced in a Cairo magazine in December 1993 that he would do the unthinkable — visit Israel. He was fifty-seven, a humorist and playwright with a popular following in Egypt. The announcement shocked Egypt's intelligentsia. Ali was known for allegorical satires of Arab governments, but he had never before ventured into the arena of Arab-Israeli relations. He was breaking the rule forbidding contact with "the Zionist entity," a rule strictly followed by all of Egypt's cultural groups and professional associations.

The response was swift. He was warned by the writers union, shunned by his colleagues, and attacked in the Egyptian press. Nevertheless, five months later in April 1994, he visited Israel. Ali's account of his trip, *A Drive to Israel*, was published by *al-Akhbar al-Youm* in October 1994. It became a bestseller among the Egyptian reading public, going through two editions.

Why did Ali Salem break the taboo on visiting Israel, and do so in this public fashion? First, he shared in the widespread burst of optimism following the September 1993 signing of the Oslo Accords between Israel and the Palestine Liberation Organization. Many Arabs (and Israelis too) were convinced at the time that with the Palestinian problem on its way to resolution, the chief obstacle to full peace between Arabs and Israelis would be removed.

The euphoria was to be short-lived. Shortly after Ali's trip, the mainstream Arab literary establishment, led by Syrian poet Nizar al-Qabbani, threatened Arab intellectuals and governments against "scurrying" towards relations with Israel. In April 1994 when Ali drove across the Sinai border, he knew Arab intellectuals remained extremely hostile to his venture.

His second reason for the visit was the conviction that by the early 1990s the Arab-Israeli conflict needed to be downgraded for internal Arab reasons. The small group of Arab liberals to which Ali belongs saw the conflict as diverting intellectual and material resources away from the real challenge ahead: democratic reform in Egypt and the rest of the Arab world. Ali hoped his visit would help dispel on the Arab side some of the inter-communal myths, and help re-focus Arab energies.

The third reason for his visit was curiosity. By 1994, despite fifteen years of formal peace between the two countries, there was still little real information about Israel available in Egypt. Ali wanted to learn firsthand about this mysterious neighbor.

Israel had appeared briefly as the mythical sphinx in one of Ali's earliest and best plays, a 1970 adaptation of *Oedipus Rex*, written in colloquial Egyptian Arabic and entitled "You are the One who Killed the Monster." His Oedipus is the charismatic leader of the ancient Egyptian capital of Thebes. Oedipus first gains renown by solving the riddle of a monster who was decimating the city's population. The city's priesthood and security chief control the city through this cult of Oedipus. But when a new monster from the desert appears outside the city gates, the people are unprepared for the coming struggle and deluded by the cult's mythologies, which require that Oedipus once again save them by fighting the monster. In the end, Oedipus is disillusioned with the people's failure to act for themselves. The monster remains triumphant outside the city gates. In this social satire of Nasser's Egypt, the monster — Israel — remaines offstage. Twenty-five years later in *A Drive to Israel*, the monster moves to center stage, and the new hero venturing off to face it is Ali himself.

Ali may be the only writer to date to uncover elements of humor in the Arab-Israeli peace process. His irreverent attitude is rooted in the mannerisms of the Egyptian theater, where he started as a comic actor in the early 1960s. The bluff public persona, however, does not conceal his brave decisions as a writer, particularly in *A Drive to Israel*.

Writing is a dangerous profession in Egypt. Two years before Ali's visit to Israel, in April 1992, Islamist terrorists shot and killed one of their main critics in Cairo, a college professor named Faraj Fouda. In October 1994, six months after Ali's visit, an Islamist militant approached Egypt's most famous novelist, Naguib Mahfouz, on a Cairo street and wounded him with a knife stab to the neck. Since writing *A Drive to Israel*, Ali has been subject to a less violent but still threatening form of reprisal, from a different quarter: the literary establishment. Egyptian and other Arab writers periodically resuscitate the charge that he is working for the Israelis, that he is betraying his country.

The charge was dusted off in the summer of 2000. Ali's script for a short film urging Egyptians to vote (entitled "Enter as a Partner and Participate") was confiscated, the film's producers were arrested, and Ali's ties to Israelis were highlighted once again in the Egyptian press. In May 2001, the Egyptian writers union took the final step of expelling Ali for advocating normalization with Israel. Undeterred, Ali Salem fights against a climate of fear that prevents Arab-Israeli contacts, and he does so in his own light, playful style.

This translation benefited greatly from the help of many teachers, friends and colleagues whom it is my pleasure to acknowledge. Laila Shaker was present from the beginning. She introduced me to Ali, then read the draft chapter by chapter, offering numerous improvements and a great deal of encouragement. Ami Ayalon, an old friend and college professor, was also a wonderful editor. Martin Kramer was the first to read the manuscript and recommend that it be published. Bernard Lewis was the first to recommend that I read Ali Salem. Sasson Somekh shared his insights into Arabic literature. Reno Harnish and Janet Silverman made valuable comments. I wish also to thank my many teachers of Arabic whose labors on my behalf over the years must have seemed in vain. Finally, this translation would not have been possible without the support of Young-Mi Silverman, who lived with me and Ali Salem's travelogue for almost one year. It is dedicated to her.

Robert J. Silverman

Going Forth from Egypt

The road to al-Arish was long and desolate, the car radio wasn't working. My only companions were my anxiety and the bothersome noise of the car engine. I was alone for long stretches of road, no one passed me in either direction. The landscape was desiccated, no one to save me if the car broke down, no hope even of encountering a highway robber.

I was exhausted, having run around since the morning to complete final errands, change the motor oil, check the tire pressure. Downtown Cairo had been crowded. I had parked the car with my bags packed, in front of the garage across from the Cairo Atelier, and went to buy a suit. I also needed some car parts. Oh skip it, I told myself, I will not use them if the car breaks down. Should I at least buy a red triangle to place near the car to warn others? Forget it, my heart told me, the car won't break down, it must know of my extreme circumstances. I likewise trusted in Chief Mechanic Osman, godfather to my green Niva, which I consider the most durable legacy of the Soviet Union. Osman had undertaken a complete overhaul of the engine. I had asked him to change any part on which he had any doubts.

"Osman...I want you to prepare this car for a long trip."

"Where'r you going?"

"To Israel."

***

At the end of 1993, directly after the declaration of the Oslo Accords between the Israelis and Palestinians, I declared an intention to visit Israel in my car to write a book answering two questions: Who are these people? What are they doing?

I published an article in *al-Shabab* magazine with the title "Peace Now." I viewed the agreement as embodying a rare moment in history, the moment of recognition of the other. I exist, and you also exist. I have a right to live, and this is also your right. It's a hard and long road, ending in freedom and human rights of the individual, a road strewn not with roses but with struggle and patience. But talking about peace isn't enough to create it. We must go forward to embody it in action, not with words.

I was completely exhausted and the road to al-Arish was still long. I had left downtown Cairo at three in the afternoon and arrived at the beginning of the road to the Suez Canal one hour later.

Obtaining a visa to enter Israel had taken only minutes at the Israeli Embassy. Yaacov Setty, the press attache, had asked me: "Do you want to visit certain areas or certain persons?"

"Sir, I will travel in my car with money in my pocket. I want to see Israel with my own eyes."

He's probably a Jew of Egyptian origin, I thought, since he spoke with me in the Egyptian dialect. Clearly he was raised on the language. But I learned later that he's of Iraqi origin. He left me for some minutes and returned to say: "The Ambassador is in a meeting now. We notified him that you came to obtain a visa and he informed us that he would like to see you for five minutes after you return."

"With pleasure."

"I also called the Rafah border crossing point...there's an amount you must pay to insure the car."

"How much?"

"Several hundred dollars."

Yaacov probably misunderstood the amount and it turned out to be less than one hundred dollars. I can't describe the consulate as opulent, but my first impression was of the quick pace of work. Yaacov left me for ten minutes, enough time to prepare the visa, pass a message to the Ambassador and receive a response, and have a quick talk with the border point at Rafah.

The only Egyptian procedure required to take my car out of the country was Form 126 of the Customs Authority. This form requires one to list all the details about the car and undertake to return it to Egypt, or else to pay its cost to the Egyptian Government. The cost of my car as determined by the Customs Authority was 17,000 Egyptian pounds.[1]

This car, purchased with my own money after paying the government all the required customs taxes, is as much mine as my pants, my shoes or my watch. It's my right to take it to Hell and do with it as I wish.

No...it is a part of Egypt's national wealth. This is a procedure left over from a totalitarian regime that views all things and persons as part of the national wealth belonging to the government, I mean "the State," I mean "the People." Most likely it is a procedure guaranteeing one's own return, a procedure still in force from the era when international air travel required the approval of the Prime Minister's office.

On my way to the Customs office in the Nasr City district of Cairo I had been absent-minded and missed the turn-off to the overpass. I began to circle the streets in a strange absent-mindedness, failing several times to take the road leading to Nasr City. I began to notice a violent, subconscious resistance to the journey. My nervous and psychological systems were undoubtedly full of fear and hatred. My conscious self wanted to go there, but subconsciously I was refusing to go. It's a heavy, life-long legacy of hatred and enmity.

This is what made me stick to car travel. If I were to travel by plane, I would find myself there suddenly, and I feared this suddenness. There was an officer in President Sadat's bodyguard who died of a sudden heart attack after reaching Jerusalem during Sadat's trip. All the news agencies agreed to keep the matter quiet. I believe his conscious failed to convince his subconscious of the new reality. The hatred inside him was too great for his nervous system to tame.

The Customs official had asked me: "Where do you work?"

"I don't have a workplace...I don't belong to any organization...I am an independent writer."

"Well, you must write for a newspaper or journal."

"Yes...for the Caricature Magazine."

"Okay then. Ask them to write a pledge document guaranteeing the return of your car."

I left the Customs a bit sad. How can I ask the owners of the magazine to guarantee the return of my car? This is my own adventure, I bear sole responsibility...what's the solution?

Why go to a senior official? I went next to the low-level employee who handles such operations. As it turned out, there was no problem. The only requirement was my personal guarantee, which sufficed. Then why had the more senior official required a guarantee from a workplace, committee, establishment or company?

The reality is that it's difficult for the government leadership to acknowledge the existence of the individual human being, that life is composed of individuals and the rights of individuals. No, for them life has a comprehensive meaning. Ministries, establishments, directorates, committees, and work forces — these are small gears turning in the great machine. It's difficult for them to imagine life beyond a public sector which denies the responsibility of individuals and the existence of their freedoms. Add to all this his lack of sympathy for my journey to Israel. Like me he is full of hatred. He imagines that I am on a journey of love, rather than a serious attempt to rid myself of this hatred. I had asked him: "When I obtain this guarantee from the management of the magazine, will you not request of me a letter of guarantee from the bank?"

He answered curtly: "This guarantee does not rule out any other procedure that might be required." The reply was vague, neither yes nor no...He merely tried to intimate that my problem was big and complicated. The reality is that the only requirement was a personal guarantee.

The road was desolate and the growing darkness increased its desolation...I was exhausted and the road to al-Arish was still long.

***

Al-Arish was getting closer. I filled up the gas tank at a station on the outskirts of town. Then I resumed driving. Al-Arish has practically no tourists at this time of year. I entered a spacious reception hall in one of the hotels, the Semiramis, and asked to phone my family in Cairo. My younger daughter answered. "Mona...I am calling from Egypt."

"From where in Egypt?"

"From al-Arish...Tomorrow morning I will go to Israel."

She screamed: "Without telling us?"

"I am sorry...Here now I am telling you...Rest assured that I am fine, all is well."

She controlled herself and said: "Okay Daddy... Come back safely."

The telephone call increased my depression and made me more tense. I knew that I was causing my daughters and wife a large amount of pain and anxiety. But I also knew that their tough advocacy against the trip would have resulted in a nervous strain that in the best of circumstances would have stripped me of the self-control necessary for the trip. It's difficult if not impossible to go forward in this life without causing some amount of pain to those we love.

I wandered the streets of al-Arish looking for a pharmacy. I bought a razor, toothbrush and paste. Am I lacking something? Yes..."No flu" pills, they relax me and I occasionally use them as a sedative. I was hungry, there was a coffee house and adjoining restaurant. I had dinner, *ful* and *ta'miya,*[2] two TV sets were placed several feet apart, one playing a foreign film with a weak picture and the other a local program with a worse picture. The sound was distorted and loud...screaming, really screaming. People on the sidewalk were staring silently at the two sets, listening to the screaming.

I felt a need to go to the bathroom. I must postpone the need until I return to the hotel, the hotel is near, I told myself...No...I can't wait. Fortunately I found a small toilet in the restaurant, paid the bill, got in the car and drove to the hotel which was only three minutes away or less. Again I felt the need to go to the bathroom, parked in front of the hotel and was propelled into my room. Oh my God, I almost lost my self-control. What has happened to me? Do I have diabetes? Until now neither my faculties nor my car has let me down, now my body? I feel the need to go to the bathroom every few minutes. What will I do tomorrow at the border Customs inspection? I do not know how I slept that night but I awoke a few times to enter the bathroom.

At about eleven o'clock on Thursday morning, 7 April 1994, I drove from al-Arish to Rafah. Feeling thirsty, I put a bottle of water in the car. I discovered after drinking I had a strong need to urinate...

The road from al-Arish to Rafah was about fifty kilometers, and I divided the road into several bathroom stops. It's best to choose a place on the side of the road that suits you, and then continue more comfortably on your way.

You are approaching the border...stop drinking...

But I feel thirsty, my throat is dry.

This thirst won't kill you...you must appear in control and natural at the Customs.

Suddenly I shouted to myself: Listen...get control of yourself. Do you hear? Get a grip on yourself.

I was speaking to my body. I knew that there is an internal power that comes out when one shouts. It is the secret of the shouts of karate masters and weight lifters. So I began to shout to my body savagely: Shut up...Think...Control yourself...Be a man... Understand?...Listen...I won't permit you to lose control...Understand?...Hey... Ah...Ahh...Aow.

It's strange but after this I began to feel more in control.

There's the barbed wire surrounding the Customs at Rafah. I parked at the gate...

"Passport please."

"Here it is."

"Are you alone?"

"Yes..."

There were huge buses in the Customs parking lot that drop off tourists on the Egyptian side, with other buses to take them to the Israeli side. I filled out a departure form at the passport window and gave my passport to the pertinent officer...

"Please sit down for a few minutes."

I sat down in the large Customs waiting room. A dark-skinned youth in shirt and pants approached: "Welcome Mr. Ali...Why don't you have a cup of coffee with me?"

In his office I drank a soft drink and talked about the reason for my visit to Israel. He handled the conversation in a friendly manner, without accusation or suspicion. He completely avoided the subject, and began to write down the outline of our conversation quickly on a piece of paper in front of him. I didn't feel angry, I appreciate that security awareness should remain active on the Egyptian-Israeli border for many years to come. Not because we are in a state of war, and not because the peace agreements we've signed are intended for appearances sake only, as if they are tactical steps in preparation for executing a final strategy of getting rid of the other. Rather, because the possibility of undermining the peace exists among numerous elements on both sides.

Many passport employees asked me the same question, I believe out of curiosity rather than for security reasons. The strangeness of the journey awoke within them a large amount of caution and wariness. Many officers came out of their offices to take a look at me, then returned to their offices. In the end, a soldier appeared carrying my departure card: "Mr. Ali...How come you're going to Israel?"

"I want to see it."

My reply made him feel perplexed. He was silent a while thinking in confusion then said: "You mean tourism?"

"Yes."

"Because you wrote the word 'visit' in the space for reason for trip...you should write 'tourism.'"

"Well, visit, tourism, what's the difference?"

The passport procedures ended and I took my passport stamped with an exit stamp and entered Customs. I was clearly the only customer in the automobile section for a number of months. The requirement was to make a photocopy of Form 126 after it was stamped, the stamp being on the back of the form. It was necessary to photocopy the form back and front. Oh...Where does one find a photocopy machine here? And if one finds it, who will permit me to make a photocopy? "Don't worry, we will copy it for you."

I sat chatting with the employee in his office while he took down the car data in a notebook. Two Customs employees appeared requesting that I go to the office of Mr. Hamdy, Director of Customs. The man welcomed me and asked if I'd like a cup of coffee. A long conversation passed between us on common friends in the field of theater, and he sent his people to photocopy the form and pay the required fee, about 16 Egyptian pounds... The Customs procedures ended.

"Is that all?"

"That's all."

"Anything else required of me?"

"Nothing, have a safe trip."

"Where do I go out?"

"From here...this way."

I started the engine and drove down the road they had indicated. Now I was crossing the border, Egypt was behind me, for a long time I wouldn't use the Egyptian dialect that I love.

I approached the Israeli military checkpoint on the border. Extremely slowly and calmly I approached the horizontal barrier. I moved forward towards taut faces covered behind dark sunglasses, some of them with long beards, and machine guns that I imagined were bigger than necessary. It is clear they chose these individuals carefully, I thought, with gigantic bodies and neat clothing...I am not watching a film in which the camera approaches an Israeli military checkpoint, I myself am actually approaching. I am watching it through the car window in front of me, not through a cinema or TV screen.

A high degree of tension prevailed at the checkpoint as I approached it. I was overcome with the feeling that any false movement on my part would result in their pulverizing my car. There are rules for approaching a military checkpoint, that is, one must stop some meters away from it. I wasn't aware of this until the front of my car was almost touching the black and yellow horizontal barrier. I was keen to show that my hands were clearly on the steering wheel. I slowly and calmly took off my sunglasses to suggest composure.

An enormous soldier came forward from the barrier while a number of others drew back and assumed ready positions. He raised high his right arm and signaled that I should pull back. His signal was closer to a parade ground command, as if he were signaling to a large corps of cars. His signal also carried the meaning of a rebuke for my getting too close to the barrier. I pulled back a few meters and he opened the barrier towards me. At that moment I felt the need to break the air of extreme tension that had unnecessarily prevailed. Silence sometimes makes people feel frightened. I asked in a raised voice: "Hey...does anyone speak English?"

"Yes...Where are you going?"

"To Israel..."

A soldier approached me and I showed him my passport. Social practice in Egypt in such circumstances would dictate that I get out of the car, but here it would have been dangerous to do so unless requested of me. Finally he indicated that I should open the hood of the car, so I got out of the car. He glanced at the engine, then used an instrument to check for explosives, took a quick glance at the contents of the car while one of his colleagues spoke on a walkie-talkie. I could see the parking lot of the Customs exactly behind the barrier at a distance of about a hundred meters. The parking lot was empty. Then someone exited the Customs building into the parking lot. Clearly he was waiting for me.

They asked me to go to the parking lot through the side road, not through the checkpoint gate. The man was indeed waiting for me. He was wearing a gray uniform, a security man. He asked me to leave the car and walk with him. I began to lock the car door but he requested that I leave it open and not to fear for it.

I entered the passport hall with him, proceeded to the window behind which was seated a young police woman. She gave me an entry card to fill out and asked: "What hotel are you staying at?"

"I have not made any hotel reservations."

"Where are you going in Israel?"

"To every place and all places."

"Whom do you know there?"

"The Mayor of Nazareth Tawfiq Ziyad, the novelists Emile Habibi and Sami Michael, and Professor Sasson Somekh who is head of the Arabic literature department at Tel Aviv University."

A young man in jeans was standing next to me. At first I thought he was a traveler until I noticed the small walkie-talkie in his hand. He said to me in English: "I am responsible for security here...I would like to speak with you a little."

In quick short sentences, I informed him of who I was and the aim of my visit.

"Do you have with you any weapons of self-defense?"

"No."

"Did anyone give you anything?"

"No."

He summoned one of his assistants, an Arabic speaker, who filled out the required forms relying on the data on my Egyptian car license. There was no importance to the Egyptian Customs' coupon-book for which I paid 260 Egyptian pounds; they didn't require it. I began to move from one employee to another, changed $500 into shekels. The shekel was about 1.25 Egyptian pounds, the dollar was less than three shekels. I paid insurance to cover car accidents for a period of one month, they gave me a license to drive in Israel. The administrative procedures ended.

Once again the security official went out with me to the area where my car was parked. "Now take out all of your belongings and place them on the trolley."

I had imagined that they would inspect my suitcases in the car. I had actually transformed the car into a big suitcase with my things thrown into every corner in plastic sacks. I placed them all on the trolley, took it to the Customs hall, and went back to the car with the official. He asked me to drive it onto a mechanic's pit with stairs. He descended the stairs and inspected the underneath of the car, came back up and asked me to open the hood. He must have been shocked at the condition of the engine, which hadn't been cleaned for months. It did not inspire confidence. He was silent a while, no doubt searching for a description that would not make me feel insulted. Finally he said: "The engine is covered with dust."

In reality I intentionally didn't clean the car, as the saying goes, "Better to leave the mud on, than to wash it off in a dirty pond." I feared that washing it with water would risk exposing the distributor cables and spark plugs to destruction. He checked every part of the car with an anti-explosive device. I returned to the Customs building through the exit this time. They had almost finished inspecting my belongings when I returned to my car... An Arabic-speaking Customs employee gave me a map. I gave him a quick glance, indicating I am not trained to follow directions on a map, road signs written in English work for me.

"Take this road...you will find the border crossing point, take a right...then continue on the road. Pay attention to the signs."

"Thanks."

I set out on the road to Tel Aviv, in my car with its Cairo license plates bearing white Egyptian numerals on a black background.

Later Victor Nachmias, a Jew of Egyptian origin, told me: "Look, you neglected to mention your wandering around here in a car with Egyptian plates. I don't know whether you are aware of it or if it's residing in your subconscious. You are roaming the streets of Israel raising the Egyptian flag."

I wasn't thinking of this, but I admit it: when they left me the Egyptian plates, I felt happy. And I began to exploit the opportunity to announce my nationality, particularly in Israeli Arab villages...With Egyptian plates and a high-pitched jeep engine I was shouting, without opening my mouth: Hey, folks!...Egypt is your neighbor...I am an Egyptian coming forth from Egypt.

Sir, I Got Lost

The landscape was similar on both sides of the border for a great many kilometers. Sand dunes with bits of green obstinately creeping forward, though the predominant color was yellow. The further I penetrated into Israel, however, the more the color green became victorious. Yellow began a withdrawal announcing its defeat before the will of humankind, while yet returning to confront green from time to time and in sector to sector, in order to remind you of the most dangerous problem of the region: water.

I began to read the signs: Ashdod, Ashkelon, Beer Sheva, the signs are written in Hebrew and English. They were written in Arabic only near Arab towns. My childhood awoke: These are the names which filled the radio news bulletins in 1948. The road I am driving on now is the road on which Egyptian trucks and armored vehicles drove before, in a war the true details of which are still unknown today.

The traffic was not heavy in this area, only enormous tourist buses heading toward the Egyptian border or coming from it. Dozens of names of "moshavot" and small farms which I hadn't known or heard of before. The unknown surrounded me and I drove toward the unknown. We don't use the seatbelt when driving in Egypt, but one must use it here. I had thoroughly cleaned the belt which had transformed over the years into a belt of dust, confirmed that it would work, and determined to use it after crossing the border. It's strange that I had forgotten to use the belt and didn't notice it until reaching the outskirts of Tel Aviv.

I was still on a secondary road which hadn't intersected with the highway. I drove the car at a steady speed, less than a hundred kilometers per hour, the traffic had begun to increase with many cars coming up behind me. The drivers were eager to read the license plate on my car, some of them were near-sighted to the extent that they almost touched my car from behind.

A strange sight, I thought, all the cars have their lights on. It's a bright and clear day and we are still hours from sunset. Why do they have their lights on?

I later learned the answer. They say this lessens accidents, it's not an optional matter, rather the law requires it except during the summer months.

The effort and loneliness, the constant speed, the high-pitched sound of the engine and unchanging features of the road together made me succumb to a kind of torpor very near to sleepiness.

There finally was a gas station, every gas station in Israel has a small cafeteria. The station was not on my right but on the left across the road. No matter, I stopped on the right side, checking to make sure there was no one behind me or coming in the opposite direction, and that the island between the lanes was fit for crossing. I turned around carefully from the extreme right to the extreme left and entered the station. I later learned that I had committed a large traffic stupidity. A great many accidents are caused by this act, it isn't permitted to cross the road except at an intersection. I asked to fill up the gas tank.

The gasoline was 91 or 96 octane. No matter, I decided, the 91 octane is only one degree different from the gasoline used in Egypt. There is no need to confuse the carburetor with a very different type of gasoline. I must have lost a lot of time at the two Customs inspections at the border since the time is now three-thirty in the afternoon.

I noticed that I hadn't eaten since breakfast, so I entered the cafeteria and asked for a sandwich, can of soda water, cup of coffee and bottle of water to drink on the road. I paid about 30 Egyptian pounds. There's no need to calculate the amount in Egyptian pounds and thus feel frustrated, I thought. Calculate it in shekels. The Egyptian pound, despite all the accusations leveled against it, is capable of buying tangible things, for example, at least four governmental and opposition newspapers. Meanwhile the shekel is incapable of moving on its own, it is constantly in need of companions. You can't buy anything with one shekel, except a pocket pack of facial tissues.

A liter of 91 octane gas cost 1.86 shekels, more than two Egyptian pounds. Near the gas pump was a pickup truck whose owner was wearing an Arab galabiya, jacket and headdress. I asked him about the road to Tel Aviv and he described it to me. I didn't need to ask him since I had earlier asked the station attendant, but it seemed that I wanted to speak Arabic.

Once again on the road, feeling full, more active and awake, I observed a private car staying behind me at a constant speed. From the rearview mirror I noticed its four occupants were wearing military uniforms. The car disappeared after a short while... Whenever I was in doubt about the direction of the arrow in the road signs, especially at intersections, I stopped to ask some other drivers, until I exited onto the highway.

I am not so stupid as to imagine that I am far from the eyes of Israeli security, in a country whose prime obsession is security. I would likewise be mentally deficient were I to imagine that my travels in Israel were far from the eyes and ears of Egyptian intelligence. Sometimes the only indication of the presence of security is an unusual, clear absence of security. A strange car with black license plates, the color used by West Bank vehicles. And no police car stops to check it the whole road from Rafah to Tel Aviv?

The woman officer at the passport control had had what is called a "watch list." She spoke with me in a cold, indifferent manner as if she did not know anything about me. I noted however that while writing, she was humming a song in a low tone. This is a mental trick intended to disguise a state of excitement in circumstances such as these. "I must appear unconcerned and calm, I will be so natural and indifferent as to sing...do you not hear me singing?"

The security officer in the Customs, called the "station manager," was also awaiting my arrival, which was not a secret since I informed the Embassy of the date of my travel. The security officer has no interest in politics or diplomacy, in war or peace. His modus vivendi is precision, doubt, and suspicion, and thus he didn't say: "Welcome, right this way...we know that you have come on a journey of peace." Instead he subjected my car and my effects to the strictest search and inspection that simplicity and manners would allow.

We all remember Sadat's historic trip. At the time, Israeli security posed a strange question: What if Sadat's plane lands, its doors open and out comes a squad of Egyptian commandos with machine guns, to mow down all the leadership of Israel gathered on the tarmac? Of course it was a silly and remote, indeed impossible, scenario. Nevertheless, they took it into consideration, and posted a number of special operations men on the rooftops of the airport buildings in order to handle such a scenario. There is a simple rule in the security field: no surprises.

On the highway, I told myself I would not turn left or right until I find the road into Tel Aviv. Then I will drive along the streets until I find a parking place where I will stop, get out and look for a hotel.

Tel Aviv drew near, people were waiting at bus stops, there were many exits with names I have never heard of. Oh wretched ignorance, I am not trained to use highways, they don't enter cities but circle around them. Thus I found myself passing Tel Aviv onto the road to Haifa. Small cities off to the left and the right and I didn't know the road. Okay, pull over on the right — I told myself — until a police car arrives or until you are able to ask a passerby. But there was no place where I could pull over. Road maintenance work underway left no room for one to park. The traffic was fast and also insane.

Darkness began to fall, everyone was driving as if fleeing from a disaster. Darkness added to the unknown, a feeling of depression swept over me interspersed with flashes of brutish pleasure. Oh my God, I am exhausted and lost in a strange country. I dreamt of a bed and going to the bathroom. At one of the stop lights, I asked the driver of a pickup beside me: "Excuse me...I want to get to any city...is Haifa far?"

"An hour from here."

"What is the closest city?"

"Netanya...about twelve kilometers away."

"Okay, I would like to go to Netanya."

"Follow me."

My memory summoned an article I had read years ago in a Qatari magazine, an illustrated investigative report written by one of the magazine's Palestinian editors, a visit to Israel and his family in the West Bank. I recalled that he visited Netanya...a phrase from it sprang to mind, "by the beautiful beach of Netanya." And then the complete sentence began to waft upwards into my memory: "By the beautiful beach of Netanya I found a comely police officer in a bikini with a pistol belt around her midriff."

It appears that the novelty of the imagery had kept it in my memory. Certainly the beach is still in its place, but what about the comely police woman? Is she still there in her bikini since the date the article was written? Has she put her clothes back on and returned home, or has she moved to another beach? Perhaps she has left the service. Tomorrow, God willing, I will search the beach for the answer.

I kept behind the pickup for several kilometers, then he indicated by his rear lights that he would pull over to the right. I parked behind him. He got out holding a pen and paper and drew me a quick map: "At the next traffic light, don't follow me. Take a left, I will continue on to Haifa.

After the light you'll find yourself on a bridge, go straight... you'll enter Netanya...there are many hotels on the beach."

"Three stars?"

"Near the beach you will find a big square for pedestrian traffic. On the right of the square are three-star hotels, on the left are five-star hotels..."

He waved goodbye at the traffic light, I turned left, over the bridge. Praise God, I am driving in a city, human beings, sidewalks, stores, buildings, lights, people walking and driving amiably. Netanya was a tourist city, a beach resort of calm and beauty. So that you understand the extent of its inhabitants' peace of mind, let me fill you in: they work in the diamond industry.

A police car was parked on a raised spot on the right. I stopped next to it. "Sirs, I am an Egyptian looking for a hotel." I extended my hand with my passport and temporary driver's license. "Stay behind these cars, they will lead you to the street parallel to the beach. There you will find a number of hotels."

I stayed behind the cars, turning first left then right, then suddenly came upon the magical word "hotel." Another miracle occurred, I found a parking space on the sidewalk next to the hotel.

I entered the hotel and asked about the closest restroom. The reception clerk was of Tunisian origin. I used a few words in Arabic and others in English: "Am I permitted to leave my car in the space in which I parked?"

"Yes."

A heavy weight dropped from my shoulders. I continued the questions: "I would like to reserve a room for two nights. How much?"

"Sixty dollars per night."

"Really...sixty? Isn't this a three-star?"

"No...four."

"It looks like three...Okay, take off a star for my sake... I thought a room at the hotel would go for only thirty dollars."

"The rates are fixed by the government."

"Hey, do you believe the government?"

The joke did not appear to amuse him, his face remained frozen. "Okay, give me a little discount."

"Fifty-five."

In reality, if he had asked for one hundred dollars I would have paid it immediately. The first night in a foreign country always costs a lot. I filled out the hotel registration form and went up to my room. I didn't tip the bell boy, I still didn't know the tipping rules here. By the time I learned them I had left the hotel. Finally here was a bed and a bathroom. I took off my clothes. The ring of the telephone surprised me.

"Hello."

"There is a man waiting downstairs who wants to talk to you."

Oh my Lord...How did they find out so quickly? The Israeli press in its special way must have learned I am at the hotel. I told him I had taken off my clothes...I will take a bath and come down in ten minutes.

I took a hot shower and changed clothes and went down to the reception. The press wasn't waiting for me, the police were faster. I found a policeman holding a hotel form.

"Yes sir..."

"There are things left in your car."

"They're books."

"Yes, I know they're books."

He checked the registration form against the passport, discovered that a number wasn't correct. "This number isn't correct."

"Yes sir, it's not correct. The person responsible for writing the error is not me but the hotel reception clerk. I didn't fill out this form...I filled out another. That one. I wrote the passport information correctly as you see."

Speaking in Hebrew, the clerk confirmed my account with some embarrassment. I felt a degree of gratification and *schadenfreude*, for the heavens had quickly punished him for not granting me the appropriate discount, especially during this dead tourist season.

The officer wrote a number of sentences in large Hebrew lettering, then signed it and said to me: "Put this on the inside of your front windshield. I will read to you what is written on it: 'The owner of this car is an Egyptian residing in the hotel. Any questions should be directed to the hotel reception.'"

I thanked him and attached the paper to the windshield...It settled the issue completely and was sufficient to fend off both policemen and the curious.

On the evening of the following day, I was sitting at the hotel cafeteria sipping a cup of black filtered coffee and chatting with some Dutch tourists when a handsome man appeared. He said to me in Arabic that he was the official of the tourist company that came with this group. He gave me the names and addresses of a great many hotels in many cities, then suddenly asked me with interest: "But why Netanya?"

At that moment an image was engraved in my mind of an official somewhere. He doesn't leave his office after being assigned to answer this question: "Why did Ali Salem go to Netanya and not to Tel Aviv?"

I sipped the coffee with relish and answered: "Sir, I got lost."

Jaffa

The evening I reached Netanya on my way to the hotel, I noticed a young boy standing at a traffic light. He was darting quickly behind cars and affixing stickers to rear windows. He's going to put a sticker on my car, I thought, and there's a slogan written on it. The situation would be of the utmost irony were it to turn out to read "Get rid of the Arabs," or some such thing. I also noticed that the boy was exchanging a few quick words with the drivers and deduced that he was asking: "Do you support this?" or "Do you agree with this?"

Some drivers indicated that they didn't agree, and the boy moved quickly to the next car. Praise God, I won't be exposed to this ordeal, I thought when the light changed, and I moved forward. At the next light, there was another boy passing out the same stickers. He said something to me in Hebrew and I responded in English: "What does this sentence say?"

"The people in the Golan."

"What about them?"

It appeared that his English wasn't up to this, so I repeated the question: "Do you want them here..."

"Yes."

Praise the Lord, so he wants an Israeli withdrawal from the Golan.

"Okay, put it on."

Thus I contributed to political work before I had placed my foot on the ground of Israel. Later I discovered that the sticker read "The prople are with the Golan," a vague formulation that had the opposite meaning to what I had intended. He was "With the Golan" in the sense that he didn't want to withdraw from it. And I as an Arab am "With the Golan" in the sense that I would like him to withdraw. In order not to produce extraneous political complications in the region, I removed the sticker.

The most interesting point is that the young boy, in that brief moment after a driver told him he didn't agree with the slogan, did not feel angry or frustrated. Instead he quickly moved on to another car. The boy did not scream: "You creep, why don't you agree?...You must be an agent of the Syrians and the Arabs."

We must focus on this point in raising our children. It is a person's right to hold different views and ideas, as long as he doesn't espouse violence or aggression. Let ideas do combat with each other, theory against theory, for the benefit of the nation.

Public debates here are not confined to the offices of political parties or newspaper columns. You see them transformed into banners held by groups of young men and women on street corners. Sometimes you find a demonstration of two persons carrying a banner announcing their joint political position. There is a well-known group that stands on a certain street corner in Jerusalem wearing black clothes and holding signs saying: "Leave the West Bank...Leave the Golan...Leave Gaza."

You will find another group in the middle of Jerusalem raising signs saying: "The West Bank begins here," meaning that if we vacate the West Bank, we'll wind up withdrawing from Jerusalem.

A single party and single ideology, especially when they are shining and idealistic, conceal sharp contradictions which are not in harmony with the laws of reality and its given quantities. These contradictions lead in the end to a big explosion. They are transformed into rockets, warplanes, tanks and casualties. People die and kill gratuitously, for no reason or for stupid ideas...ask the people of Iraq, or Kuwait, or Yemen.

***

Before I traveled to Israel, an old friend came to me and said: "I've just attended a meeting at which it was decided to purge you and your family from all literary, cultural, artistic, and social groups, if you go to Israel."

I felt a sense of disgust. What is the appropriate response in this situation? Minds raised on purges either attempt to purge enemies who hold contrary views, or their enemies attempt to purge them. These minds cannot envision that some people do not fear their threats. The success of their blackmail only hardens their resolve to have their way with all thought and action.

I responded to him: "Tell them that Ali Salem has in fact already gone. Feel free to carry out your threats."

Another friend wrote after I returned: "If we were judges, we would have put you on trial."

I reply here: A judge must be qualified, but you have none of that. Fairness is required, but you are trained in tyranny. You are a chance odd occurrence of history, a remnant at a moment when totalitarian dictatorship is ending throughout the world. You are against me because you have nothing with which to promote peace, and you didn't have anything with which to promote war other than lies and weakness.

Peace is made by the brave and you are cowards. Those who seek it are wise and free men, while you are enslaved fools. Those who work for it are strong and you are weak.

Sir, how can you dream of judging me and putting me on trial, while you still do not know the difference between freedom of expression and shamelessness, or the difference between journalism and crime!

***

I made a call from the telephone in the hotel room to Suleiman al-Fahmawi, to his village in Umm al-Fahm[3] near Nazareth. He is an engineer and owner of a construction company, he also works in the field of publishing. I made his acquaintance in the "Caroline" cafeteria when he visited Cairo for the international book fair last winter.

"Is it possible...Where are you calling from?"

"From Netanya...the Grand Metropol Hotel on Gad Machness Street."

"Gad Machness...do you know this name?"

"It's the name of a street."

"No...he's a famous football player. We already agreed before that you would come stay with me."

"God willing. I will stay here two nights, and after that I'll come to visit you, then go to Nazareth to see Samih al-Qasim, Emile Habibi, and Tawfiq Ziyyad."

"Do you know that my office is very close to Netanya? Only ten minutes away."

"Wonderful...Listen I discovered that I don't have with me the telephone number of Professor Sasson Somekh. Could you look it up and phone me back at the hotel?"

***

I went out to stroll the streets of Netanya. All the beaches in the world pretty much resemble one another. But here they strove to add human ingenuity to that of nature. A large square was infused with flowers and plants and stone benches. Dozens of small restaurants and cafes encircled the area in a pretty arrangement. As for the beach itself, you descend to it via stone works and stairs interspersed with green, as if it's a wrapping for the beach, which is presented to you on a large round stone tray.

I ate dinner. Here the lifebuoy and path to safety is *shawarma*[4], a pitta of *shawarma* the size of a small city square. After receiving it you find before you large plates full of different types of salads and pickled vegetables. You put what you like on a small plate.

At a small patisserie, I took an espresso with a piece of cake, feeling the need to spoil myself after this long journey.

It is wonderful in this era that man has found spacious places in which to walk and sit without the crowding of cars, without honking and noise. I noticed that I was the only person walking alone in the square. I was not the only one to notice it. Suddenly in front of me stopped a woman whose face was covered with makeup in an eye-catching manner. "Hi."

"Hi."

"Where from?"

"From Egypt."

"By yourself or with a group?"

"By myself."

"Work or tourism?"

"Work."

"Don't you want to sit in a nice bar?…There's a nice bar on the corner."

"Thanks. I am walking a bit and will go back to the hotel."

"Don't you want a woman?"

I felt ashamed and slightly afraid. It's repulsive for a man to tell a woman he doesn't want her, even if he doesn't know her, even if she practices the oldest profession in history. My answer must not be degrading but at the same time convincing, I told myself. I stammered out: "I really am not interested, for reasons peculiar to me and not connected with you. I mean that I am sorry."

She said as she drew away: "If you change your mind I will be at the bar on the corner."

The way she ended the encounter, preserving each party's dignity, pleased me. In these issues and in the political conflict one must always leave the door open. In reality there was nothing about her, either in appearance or content, to make anyone change one's mind.

When I returned to the hotel I found a phone message from Suleiman with Professor Somekh's phone number. I called him and spoke with his wife who welcomed me. I left a message with my address and telephone and then went to sleep.

***

Sasson Somekh is the head of the Arabic language and literature department at Tel Aviv University, and one of the most famous professors of Arabic literature outside of Egypt. He has a doctorate from Oxford University, an Iraqi Jew who came to Israel before he was twenty years of age. Sasson says Emile Habibi taught him politics and Tawfiq Ziyad taught him to drink. Arabic literature is not only his love and profession, it is also his biggest investment in peace between Arab and Jew. He has spent his entire life studying Arabic literature and has given his nation and the whole world important works on two Egyptian giants of literature, Naguib Mahfouz and Yousef Idris. He has also given the universities of the world dozens of his students who have become specialists in Arabic language and literature, including the Egyptian dialect.

Sasson's overwhelming interest in Arabic literature springs from both this desire to achieve peace between Arab and Jew, and also to achieve it between parts of himself. It is torture to be an intellectual in Israel who is both Arab and Jew at the same time. How painful it is to find yourself — for reasons not of your making — an enemy to yourself. How difficult it is for your government to make war on your identity. Thus his clear stand on the side of the Arab Palestinians caused some to accuse him of being an agent of the PLO.

I had only recently made his acquaintance. He had not read my works before we met in Cairo, about one month before my travel to Israel. We were introduced by a researcher named Raymond Stock, a regular at the soirees of Naguib Mahfouz. Sasson had invited me to dinner together with the novelist Sami Michael and one of his students, whose first name I remember was Nancy.

They were in a deep depression in the wake of the barbaric crime at the Cave of the Patriarchs in Hebron[5], which struck a bitter blow at the steps towards peace. I informed him that I would visit Israel shortly, I was on the verge of traveling if not for the barbaric crime.

Actually Sasson didn't believe me. He imagined this was merely a wish that would inevitably fail to materialize. A large number of Egyptian intellectuals had already said to him that they would visit Israel and none had come.

***

In the morning Sasson called to say that he would come by shortly. Then Karen called. She is a poet and professor of English literature at Tel Aviv University. I have known her since 1981, when we were together for two weeks at the Salzburg Seminar, sponsored by the Fulbright Commission. We were with about sixty-five professors of English and American literature from all parts of the world. Also with us was Dr. Abdel Aziz Hamoudah, the playwright, critic and former dean of literature at Cairo University. Nine years later I met her again at the University of Michigan.

Karen said: "Ali, do you have enough clothes? My son is as tall as you and is exactly your size."

"Thanks Karen...I have enough, maybe too many clothes."

Sasson probably told her that I came in my car without informing my family, meaning that I didn't have clothes. In fact I had drawn up and carried out a well thought-out plan to buy clothes before traveling. I hid them in a safe place so that when I left the house to go on the trip I appeared to have only a shirt and pants. In truth and for the sake of history, I smuggled out two pairs of shoes that morning in spite of the severe monitoring imposed on me.

Sasson came with one of his students, whom he introduced to me: "Gaby...Gabriel Rosenbaum...his doctorate is on the Egyptian theater...He teaches Arabic theater at the Hebrew University in Jerusalem. He also teaches your play 'You are the One who Killed the Monster.'"

"Nice to meet you Gaby...Your face is familiar to me... Have we met before?"

"You probably saw me at the Naguib Mahfouz soirees...or in the Odeon Cafeteria...or with Lenin al-Ramli. I am now translating his play 'Sa'adoun the Madman' into Hebrew."

Gaby spoke the Egyptian dialect well, indeed he knew all its secrets. A young man who looked old, his hair prematurely gray, sensitive and soft-spoken, he reminded you of Egyptians at their best. The permanent smile on his face doesn't leave even when he is lecturing.

Gaby asked me to visit him at the university and speak to his students, and I promised to do so when I went to Jerusalem. Gaby took off in his car and I went out with Sasson towards Tel Aviv. We went to Tel Aviv University; the guard at the gate refused to allow my car to enter since we didn't have a permit. I parked in a waiting area also belonging to the university across the street and we went on foot to Sasson's office. No one was in the university since the professors had been on strike for two months seeking higher wages.

The road from Tel Aviv to Jaffa was about twelve kilometers passing along the Mediterranean corniche. Jaffa is a city in which both Jews and Arabs live. Do I need to say that Jaffa is beautiful, and one of the most ancient ports in history?

At the entrance to the city stood a large building resembling a fortress overlooking the coast from a high hill. Dispersed around it distant from the coast were stone houses that one would think were museums owing to their extreme beauty. Inside the city the houses were modest one- or two-story buildings.

In the tourist part you feel the refreshing sea breeze has mixed with the strong smell of history. In Netanya and Tel Aviv you feel yourself in places built only yesterday; here in Jaffa you sense the glory and might of the ancient.

I had only been in three places but I began to discover the innermost secret of peace: tourism.

Tourism requires creativity no less than does war. If war is the art of destroying life, then tourism is the art of preserving it. It is the genius of administration, discipline and preservation of the environment, of beautifying and maintaining it with all the effort, strength and imagination for beauty given to man. Tourism requires discipline among the organs of society, but in turn it gives back and contributes to supporting this discipline, after the income from it is transformed into a source of strength and good for all the society's individuals. If knowledge is the single source of wealth on earth now, through which we can exploit nature's wealth for the benefit of man, and since the ancient proverb says "know yourself," then the modern proverb should be "know the map of tourism in your country and present it to others." Present it suffused with beauty and uniqueness, so that your conduct can be part of the greatness of your antiquities.

At the beginning of Yafet Street in Jaffa, the central commercial street in the city, there was a small bakery that had become a phenomenon, a tourist Mecca. Its owner was named "Abu al-Afiyah." Queues of tourists stood outside on the sidewalk eating pieces of baklava, croissants, and pastries. Through advertisements in tourist brochures, he had been transformed from a mere man who had mastered his profession into a source of natural wealth, his name exploited for tourism so that one who eats at his place imagines his health will increase.

Until now I had not seen fancy cars like the varieties of Mercedes in Cairo, despite the fact that the roads were crammed with cars the size of ships. I know that they are hiding many things from me, I thought, but how can Israeli intelligence hide these cars or remove them from my path? Or do they not drive these cars because they are stingy? Is it because they fear envy?

One should not arrive at an answer hastily, it should be left to researchers. But if I had to state my initial conclusions, I would say that luxury in Israel is a public and not a private good. They have no reason to seek to outdo their neighbors with fancy cars or homes. Even so, nearly all their cars are new and in good condition. The mountainous nature of the roads demands strong engines. In short, they use cars only as a means of transportation.

In only a very few cases did I see noticeably old cars, with the exception of course of my car which won their admiration in a special way. They could not imagine that a 1980 model is allowed to run in the New World Order. They were all keen to take a picture of me standing beside it, actually, of it standing beside me since it became more famous than I.

**

A walk through Jaffa with Sasson then dinner in an Arab fish restaurant by the coast. I ordered a small fried *barbone* (red mullet) and white rice.

I felt a bit vaguely that there was a connection stretching back over thousands of years between Damietta my home town[6] and Jaffa, and that this connection must have resulted in a similar way of cooking fish with rice. When the fish came it was as if a Damietta matron had prepared it. Afterwards, in the writer's club in Tel Aviv where Karen and her husband invited me to dinner, I ordered grilled mullet and rice. After this I confirmed that the Damietteans had been here in the distant past.

We returned from Jaffa, I left Sasson near his house in Tel Aviv and he asked me to continue on the highway to Netanya. I will not get lost this time, I thought, since I know the exit off the highway to Netanya. I entered Netanya from another exit off the highway, and found myself on a road I had never been on before. I didn't worry, the sea was to my left and the hotel was after all near the coast.

I returned by myself and arrived at the hotel feeling a certain quantity of what I had been in need of: self-confidence.

The Convent of the White Sisters

I paid the hotel bill, left the room and put my bags in a storage area behind the reception desk. I went out and walked on the beach a little, to pass the time until my eleven-o'clock appointment with Sasson and Karen. The trip to Haifa in Sasson's car lasted less than one hour. We visited two of Sasson's friends at Haifa University, Professor Yosef Ginat and his wife, who are active in the peace movement. We toured Haifa a bit. Valley dwellers feel a sense of awe when they visit cities in the mountains.

Inhabitants of the Nile Valley associate the word "mountain" with a desolate place of hunters and wild animals. Thus it is also natural that we are overcome with a certain amount of astonishment and marvel when we see mountains that have been transformed into gardens, clean streets and neat houses.

From a lookout point above the city our two guests began to describe its contours. This is the port, to the far north is the border with Lebanon. Those hills you see so clearly are the Golan Heights. I asked that we have lunch at a simple plain Arab restaurant, for in my experience, magnificent-looking restaurants that cater to tourists sell only their magnificence. The restaurant resembled a large warehouse or mess hall, merely tables and chairs, though it was full of people. It turned out to be a building of the British military command during the Mandate. *Kofta* here is called *kabab* and what we call *kabab* is here called skewered meat. In all likelihood, it will take several centuries before they will be able to produce kabab and kofta corresponding to what is served in Egypt, on condition that they hire Egyptian experts and expend intensive efforts to unify the terminology in this field.

They have a dish called *mujadarah* made of rice and black lentils. In all likelihood, this dish was frozen at a stage of evolutionary development some thousands of years ago. Had this dish been allowed to develop naturally under stable, creative living conditions, it would have evolved into the well-known Egyptian *kushary*.

What bothered me in the restaurant was the owner himself. Filling his restaurant with people had afflicted him with a kind of arrogance that made him say that he hadn't liked the food in Cairo. Each to his own.

***

We left Haifa with time enough to return to Netanya by four in the afternoon, when I was to meet Suleiman and go with him to his village of Umm al-Fahm. He said: "Stay behind me...I want you to take a careful look when we pass through Afula...We will be on the road where the incident happened two days ago."

"What incident?"

"You don't know!? A booby-trapped car collided with a bus and caused an explosion that wounded many people and killed an Arab and a Jew. A youth wired himself with a bomb and loaded his car with explosives, then stopped suddenly in front of a bus and was hit by it."

"Can't we circle around and go another way?"

"No, we must pass the same road to get to Umm al-Fahm."

The incident occurred on Wednesday, I had entered Israel on Thursday. This then is the reason for the intense tension among the soldiers at the border crossing point. This is also the reason for the tension and the aggression among some of the drivers on the road. They were honking at me when I merely approached the median strip on the highway. On the coast road from Tel Aviv to Jaffa, I felt several times from the way they were closing in on me that they wanted to force me off the road, though I was driving at the speed dictated by the pace of traffic. This is also the reason for the interest of the policeman in Netanya, and the insistence of the officer on writing a note to attach to the windshield.

My Lord, I was moving about all this time in the lap of danger without knowing it.

The car which exploded in Afula didn't have the black license plates of the West Bank, it was stolen from Israel and had yellow Israeli plates. But, as the saying goes, "those who are burned by soup blow on yogurt to cool it." And the yogurt here is my car with its black plates and Arab numerals.

In Afula a large number of youth had erected several tents on the sidewalk at the place of the incident, as if they were setting up "tents of mourning."[7] But the traffic didn't stop and they were not stopping it either. Even if an extremist had noticed my Arab car, I would have driven by before he could have thought of doing me harm. I breathed a sigh of relief when I departed Afula.

Umm al-Fahm is a small Arab town, its narrow alleys branching out up the mountain at sharp angles. How did people reach their homes here before the invention of cars? I felt at times as if I were climbing a wall with my car. You do not feel like a stranger in Umm al-Fahm since it doesn't differ greatly from any small city in the Delta provinces of Buheira or Menufiyyah.

At the entrance to the village, on a high hill, stood the village emblem, a water pitcher of stainless steel. Yes, it was indeed the pitcher of ritual ablution[8], and the village elder, who also serves as the mayor of the city, had erected it. He had also raised many small banners with religious slogans scattered throughout the village on metal poles. It was clear that some in the village disagreed with his orientation since some of the banners had been torn down. He was of course a moderate and enlightened religious man, a believer in democracy. The evidence for this was that he had obtained his position though democracy's good offices, out of his concern for the elements of life in the village, roads, education, medical facilities, cleanliness, employment. But he had confused his jurisdiction with that of the village preacher. Thus, time and a large portion of the village budget were lost in preparing its inhabitants for dealing with the afterlife, leaving interest in the life of this world to mayors of other, infidel cities.

I asked Suleiman to reserve a hotel room for me in Nazareth for a period of three nights beginning from the next morning. He looked in the telephone directory then phoned a hotel named Saint Gabriel. "Ask them how much, Suleiman."

"Thirty-five dollars."

"Too much, Suleiman...We are now in low season."

Of course I didn't know whether we were in low season or high season. But there was nothing wrong in using the term to obtain a discount.

Suleiman went on talking on the telephone: "Thirty-five is too much...Thirty is enough...What is madam's name? Maryam? Nice speaking with you Maryam. Good, we'll see you tomorrow morning."

I spent the night with Suleiman. In the morning he awoke early and, since he had work in Jerusalem, asked his brother Muhammad to drive in front of me to Nazareth. As I left Umm al-Fahm the car engine began rattling. Dust particles had caused a blockage in the muffler opening. A simple, silly defect, which nonetheless could be dangerous here. The mountain roads ascend and descend and inability to control one's car even for a moment could result in disaster.

I signaled Muhammad with flashing lights that I would stop. I asked that we go to the nearest mechanic. It took a few minutes to explain the defect to the mechanic since the terms of auto mechanics are French in Egypt, but English here. Finally he told me: "Oh...oh...you mean the muffler."

"Exactly. The muffler is what we call 'silenceur.'"

He sprayed the muffler opening with a hand air pump, checked the radiator and battery water, and brought a bottle of anti-corrosion liquid. He put a bit in the radiator and gave me the bottle, then checked the brake and clutch fluid. I also asked him to tighten the hand brake. In Egypt we rarely use the hand brake, but on mountainous roads they must be in good repair. He refused to take a single penny from me so I gave him one of my books. I often use my books as a form of cash.

Once again I passed the same ill-fated street in Afula. The traffic was stopping this time, a large crowd had gathered at the site of the incident. But I felt reassured after learning that nearby were a police station, ambulance, fire department and hospital. This had helped quickly save a large number of the victims.

**

This then is Nazareth. Her beauty, calm and goodness are drawn on the faces of her people. They are not tense or taut features.

Saint Gabriel Hotel was once a convent called the Convent of the White Sisters. It's on the summit of a mountain overlooking the city of Nazareth. Nuns usually choose an elevated and remote place on which to build their convents. Height makes one feel closer to the heavens, and remoteness embodies distancing from the sins of man.

Man multiples and advances on every site. Here the convent was losing both its remoteness and its elevation. It must become something else. I have stayed in my travels at a great many hotels, but I felt here a sense of repose which I had never felt before. It was as if the nuns had left behind their gentleness and goodness. Only one thing bothered me: I was alone.

Solitude is required for creation. But it causes one to lose any sense of enjoyment.

In the foyer a beautiful set of Arab furniture caught my eye. An Arab girl was at the reception desk.

"Are you Miss Maryam?"

"Yes."

"I am so and so. We spoke with you yesterday."

"Welcome."

"Sister Maryam...Thirty dollars is a bit much, don't you think?"

"Done, we'll leave it at twenty-eight."

"Still a bit high my dear."

She smiled gently and sweetly and said: "How much would you like to pay?"

"I'd like to pay twenty-five."

"Done...we'll leave it at twenty-five."

They treat you with generosity in this hotel. Whenever I met a hotel worker, day or night, I was asked: "Would you like a cup coffee?" They had noticed from the beginning that I am a coffee connoisseur, and they apparently feared that the high price was deterring me from ordering it. They were generally aware, from their repeated visits to Egypt, that the prices here were not appropriate for Egyptians. Incidentally, I believe that people need the highest quantity of evil to hate Egyptians. But perhaps I say this because I am Egyptian.

When I departed from the hotel Maryam said to me: "Mr. Ali, I am very sad because the hotel owner is not here. He loves Egypt very much. Of course we all love Egypt, but you cannot imagine his love. Look, this foyer furniture is from Egypt...These chairs are from Egypt...Most of the room and restaurant furnishings are from Egypt."

***

Sasson phoned to say that the newspaper *Kull al-Arab*, the editor in chief of which is Samih al-Qasim, would send its literary editor Suleiman Abu Natour to interview me. But a few minutes later a reception clerk informed me that a journalist named Fayez Abbas had phoned and was on his way.

It appeared that the literary editor had sent someone else.

Fayez came, a youth with a thick beard and sunglasses.

The thick beard and glasses transformed into a heavy mask hiding his true feelings from you. You constantly felt that he was distant from you.

"Why are you here?"

"I'm here to support the Oslo Accords, to support Palestinian-Israeli peace, and to get to know people from contact with them."

"But why did you come by car?"

"To remind people that we have a common border between us, that we are close to each other. We must make peace for the sake of the freedom of the individual, and his rights not as a Jew or Muslim or Christian or as a believer in any other religion, but as a human being."

"Was it an easy thing?"

"No, it was very difficult. Perhaps it was internal, in a repeated dream, but all that man has achieved has appeared once as an impossible dream."

Fayez invited me to lunch in the hotel restaurant but I felt like trying someplace different.

"Why don't you invite me to a restaurant in the city?"

"My time is tight, I have a lot of appointments."

"Okay, we'll be quick. But would you please deliver for me several books to Samih al-Qasim...you are returning to the newspaper of course."

"I don't work for *Kull al-Arab*."

"This wasn't an interview for *Kull al-Arab*?"

"No...For *Yediot Aharonot*."[9]

"Good... Would you mind on your way back dropping me off in front of the *Kull al-Arab* newspaper?"

His invitation for lunch evaporated with the speed of lightening, he made no effort to carry it out. He dropped me off in front of the newspaper building and pointed out the floor it occupied. Then he went on his way and I never saw him again. When I remember him, I feel amazed at not having felt any sense of friendship for him.

Samih al-Qasim is a great, well-known poet and a refined, sweet-natured, handsome person. He appears to enjoy life. He is quick-witted and has an astonishing ability to sum up his thinking. When you meet him you feel as if you have known him for a long time, as if a strong connection binds you both, a friend you have not seen in a long while. It was the first time I met him, and I liked him. Samih said: "Your intellectuals do not want to visit Israel. Who asked that they visit Israel? Visit us Arab citizens of Israel. Visit us in our homeland, we live here in our homeland. When I visited Egypt they asked for my impressions and I said I moved from one homeland to another."

We ate lunch at the Maria Fontana restaurant which had been a convent before. Samih is a person with whom you like to share a meal and drink together; it is hard to find an intellectual who opens up your appetite for food. We went back to the newspaper office. He asked Mahmoud Abu Rajab, the newspaper's secretary, to take me back to the hotel.

In the evening Mahmoud came with his wife and had a long interview with me, then they took me to Lake Tiberias.

Tourism again. It was a large lake with restaurants, hotels and casinos hugging its shores. People were partying until morning. They returned me to the hotel at one o'clock in the morning. I felt fatigue. I had a cyst on my neck which had not bothered me for months. I had forgotten it or pretended to forget it. Suddenly it was inflamed in an alarming way. I must go to a doctor, I decided. I asked Mahmoud to take me to a doctor in the morning...It appeared that I was really ill, I was not able to sleep because of the sharp pain.

Visit Us At Least Once in a Lifetime

From his office at the newspaper, Mahmoud tried to call a physician friend of his, but the line was continuously busy, so he asked me to come with him to the clinic. It belonged to the Histadrut.[10] He didn't find the physician he knew there, so I sat down to wait my turn. But he whispered into the ear of a nurse: "I have here an Egyptian colleague." The nurse took an interest. Then, the interest and enthusiasm of this nurse and the whole team of nurses and doctors ignited when he whispered into her ear, as if passing a dangerous secret: "He is the author of the play *School of the Trouble-makers.*"[11]

Despite the pain, I felt a tinge of happiness in having this experience, the experience of entering an ordinary clinic in Nazareth. It was an opportunity to get acquainted with the modern medical technology used in Israel to treat abscesses. Let's see, have they arrived at an invention to put on an abscess and make it disappear immediately? Let's see.

I pulled back the collar of my shirt and alarm appeared on the face of the doctor. He immediately prescribed two types of antibiotics, and daubed the well-known ichthyol ointment on me with a gauze bandage. It's the same ointment we use in Egypt, the only difference is that they pronounce the name *ikhthyol*. He asked that I come back at five o'clock to fill the prescriptions, since the clinic pharmacy was on a partial strike and closed during the day. However, the women doctors opened hidden drawers and swiftly took out the antibiotics. Mahmoud took me back to the hotel.

***

If Egyptian television dramas are a source for the reality of life, then there should appear at some point a beautiful blond girl named "Esther" whom the Mossad places in the way of the Egyptian hero. First she lures him into her web, then cries out of love for him...Where is she? Where is Esther?

At last Esther appeared, and with the same enchanting, celebrated specifications. She worked in the hotel and was called "Etti." She threw me several "Esther"-like glances from afar, like arrows or ground-to-ground missiles or, to be more precise, eyelid-to-eyelash missiles. I said to her: "Etti...go away from me...I am not cut to your size."

It's a famous sentence in the lexicon of courtship of the Egyptian colloquial. It appears to express a desire for distancing, while the true interpretation is that the speaker wishes to get closer. But I forgot that Esther's limited vocabulary in Arabic and experience with Egyptian colloquial didn't allow her to understand. All the hotel workers were required to participate in explaining the outward meaning of the sentence, which appeared foolish and senseless.

On the morning of the following day, I found that I was unable to change the bandage by myself. I went down to the hotel reception hall with the ointment, the gauze and the bandage. Esther was arranging the restaurant tables. "Etti, is there someone here who has a nursing background?"

She answered: "Yes, me. Come...sit here."

With trained fingers she removed the old dressing and cleaned the place, then put some ointment on a piece of gauze and attached it to my neck with the bandage. Then she departed to finish her work. If I had met "Etti" under other circumstances, on the field of battle, she would have sliced my neck with a knife or blown it off with a burst of machine gun fire. Such is man's fate on earth and his choice also, to either kill the other or dress his wounds.

This was the last scene in the drama of the trip in which Esther appeared. I apologize for disappointing the reader who perhaps had indulged in hopes of several steamy scenes in which Esther would figure. It became clear, unfortunately, that the Mossad did not instruct her to become close to me and control me. I must confess to some dereliction on my part, since owing to illness and the confines of time, I did not exert any serious effort to fall into her grasp. Generally it doesn't work dramatically or in real life for the heroine to fall in love with a hero suffering from an abscess of the neck of this size and redness. Likewise the odor of ichthyol ointment is sufficient to cause any woman to remove herself from the path of any hero.

In the evening Emile Habibi visited me in the hotel. Emile made the well-known appeal to Egyptian intellectuals: "Visit us at least once in a lifetime."[12] It is a painful appeal of both love and what appears to be the bitterness and fatigue of isolation. I met Emile for the first time at the Semiramis Hotel in Cairo, when he was invited to the Cairo International Book Fair in January 1994. I said to him: "I will visit you soon in Nazareth, Emile."

He looked at me a long while in silence as if he didn't believe me.

He invited me to dinner, but I regretted since I had an appointment with Tawfiq Ziyad who was coming in an hour. "Emile, let's wish for long lives and the chance for other visits."

Tawfiq Ziyad came. Hotel employees and people of Nazareth dining at the restaurant welcomed him warmly. I believe Tawfiq was over sixty-five years of age, but after several moments of conversation you feel his vitality and youth springing forth. He speaks in a raised voice and with elevated ideas that exactly suit his voice. He is the mayor and a member of Knesset, a courageous statesman who doesn't submit either to the blackmail of demagoguery or to the sellers of illusions. He is free of the reserve by which we know those who work in politics. The poet inside of him prevailed over the politician, or perhaps he made politics serve the concerns of poetic beauty. Since he runs a famous city, the poet is not preoccupied with the ordering of lines of verse but rather with the order-ing of daily life for the city's residents. He is responsible for transform-ing his city into a beautiful poem.

He turned to the hotel managers and said in a loud voice: "This man is my guest...Do not take money from him."

He turned to me: "Don't you dare pay for anything...you are my guest."

I almost shouted at him in exasperation: "Why didn't you tell me from the start? Why did you leave me to bargain with Maryam? You make me now regret every moment in which I resisted my desire to enter the res-taurant and bar."

Instead I shouted with an almost fake insistence: "Please Mr. Tawfiq...I beg of you...thank you very much but allow me to pay the bill, and you invite me another time."

He replied: "Let's talk of something else...Speak no more of this."

Again I shouted in a protest: "I beg of you...Leave it...Allow me to pay."

He raised his voice decisively: "No...move on...speak of another topic."

So I immediately heeded his advice and raised another topic lest he suddenly grant my request.

***

There was an urban improvements program in every street and neighborhood of Nazareth. They were preparing for the year 2000 Christmas celebration of the prophet Jesus, may God's peace be upon him. Tawfiq said to me: "My budget isn't enough for my dreams, so I recruit volunteer youth to work on some public projects...There are many young people with different specialties who work for free."

"Do you give them meals?"

"Three meals...And they work all day...We calculated the amount of work they did on one of the projects and found that it was ten times what would have been possible under the budget."

Oh...oh...oh...If only youth trust the political leadership. I didn't say it to him, I said it to myself. I hope that someone in the heavens above heard it.

"We are not going to a traditional restaurant...we will go to a place owned by a friend...we will eat fish."

"Where is this place?"

"Believe me, I don't recall the place...The last time I visited him there was years ago...But my friend will wait for us at a place nearby and lead us there."

In fact, at a place outside of Nazareth, a man was waiting in his car. We drove behind him over fields and though narrow alleys to a hut in an isolated place. The hut was narrow and the roof low. A long table completely occupied the space. There was another small room used by his friend to fry the fish, where a group of Tawfiq's friends was waiting.

The night, the man waiting for us in a car to lead us over the fields, the isolated hut with low roof, the long table with men seated around it, all these strange and obscure elements made me feel that I was acting in a film about the French resistance during World War Two, or that I was attending a meeting of a secret party.

But the fried fish was fresh and delicious. What is sweeter than friends sharing fresh fish just cooked, with juice of grape and of potato? We ate, drank, and laughed in mirth and enjoyment. There was no escape from speaking of politics. It destroys the mezze, divides the group, spoils the fish and removes the pleasant effects of the drink.

Yitzhak Rabin had issued a decree shutting off the West Bank after the explosion in Afula and other incidents. This protected — in his mind — the Israeli people. Likewise he decreed the importation of workers from outside of the region...My view was: This is a mistaken political

decision...It denies work opportunities for the Palestinians and conse-
quently turns them to poverty and misery, and transforms them into anti-
peace extremists. At the same time it doesn't protect the Israeli people.

There is nothing on earth called complete security. Rabin will not be
able to lock a security ring on the region. No curfew, however exacting
its measures, will prevent a person from slipping in a shipment of dynamite, or a revolver, or a knife. Here the pretext of protecting the Israeli
people falls. Peres says: "We must deal with poverty in the region just as
we deal with the nuclear threat." I agree with him on that. Then why does
Rabin want to cause an increase in poverty or an increase in the nuclear
threat?

The youth who committed the Afula incident was driving a car stolen
from Israel. Behind the other incident, an explosion on a bus, it turns out
there were two persons with Israeli IDs living in West Jerusalem. I say
that this decree is intended only to gratify the street, but it is a political
mistake.

"Okay...what do you say to meeting with Rabin and telling him these
words?"

"Mr. Mayor, I am not here to discuss politics. It is impolite to oppose
the decree of the prime minister of a country in which I am merely a guest.
How could I say these words to him? Were I Rabin and an Arab playwright came to me to oppose a decree of mine...I would reply to him
immediately: Brother, go be clever with the decrees of your own prime
ministers.

"There is another matter here, Mr. Mayor. I heard words here about
the importation of Egyptian laborers to work in agriculture and construction. I strongly oppose this idea...The Palestinians should work here
first...Why should we drive a wedge between the Palestinians and the
Egyptians at this heated time?"

Afterwards in Jerusalem, when I said that the decree was a political
mistake from a tactical perspective, that it aimed only to gratify the street
in Israel, Israel's former ambassador to Egypt Moshe Sasson responded
quietly: "Don't forget that it is the street which brought us to power."

Yes, this is the eternal problem of democracy and the secret of its
strength as well...But the question remains: Will the statesman lead the
street or will he be led by the street?

Dismissing the moral value in politics is an expensive political mistake. Inevitably the society pays an exorbitant bill even if only over the course of years. A few years ago politicians in Israel were saying: There is no Palestinian people...Come let's build settlements in their midst. Was that not to gratify the street? The street is not always right...Rather, it is wrong most of the time. Truth is comprehended, attained and defended by the lone intellectual. This is what your intellectuals were trying to warn of for many years.

I recall Arieh Eliav's book *Land of the Heart* written more than twenty years ago. And I recall Professor Harkavi's *Israel's Fateful Hour* written several years ago. Many voices in Israel demanded recognition of the Palestinian people and the necessity of negotiating with the Palestine Liberation Organization as the sole legitimate representative of the Palestinian people. Did the street in Israel desire it? Were they happy with it? Of course not.

Go to any street in either a backward or civilized state and say to the gathering called the masses: Let's slaughter our enemies because they are heretics...because they refuse Arab unity or because they demand Arab unity...because they are wealthier or poorer than us, because they are from the north or from the south. It is enough that they are different from us in some matter. Nothing is easier than to awaken the instinct of aggression in man.

The statesman is like a construction engineer. Will he submit to the building's owner, whose desires conflict with the rules of engineering? Will he complete the building in a defective way that will cause it to fall later on the heads of its residents? On the heads of his people?

A sentence in Eliav's book says: "We do not need to resort to violence in our relations with the Occupied Territories. Certainly this violence will be returned to us some day." No one believed him. You considered the invasion a victory...There is a unity of existence in this world. That which we do to others is precisely what we do to ourselves...Thus the value of morals in politics is not a luxury and not political stupidity, rather it is a law of existence, and the only strong basis for political work.

How can we do to others that which we hate others to do to us? What is the price we pay for committing this? I believe that the Israeli people has begun to realize now the oppressive price it is paying as a result of its politicians' ignoring for many years the existence of the Palestinian people, its rights and its identity.

***

Tawfiq brought me to the hotel at about one o'clock in the morning. I had begun to feel exhausted from the effect of the abscess and the antibiotics. I don't know how I slept.

I checked out of my room at noon, the time of my appointment with Sasson who was arriving from Tel Aviv by bus. We had agreed by telephone that we would visit some literary figures in Nazareth before heading for Tel Aviv. He was late. I learned from some people in the hotel that traffic had stopped on the Tel Aviv-Nazareth road. Two incidents had occurred — an attempted explosion on a bus, and an Arab woman stabbed three Jews. The news made me dispirited, especially since I was in a bad physical and psychological condition.

Sasson arrived at about three o'clock in the afternoon. I was unable to move. I couldn't drive my car in this condition. Oh, if only I could sleep for a few minutes...I said to Sasson: "I am very tired and in need now of a bit of rest."

"Maryam...I checked out of the room, but I need to sleep now a little."

"The whole hotel is at your service."

I went up to the room with Sasson. They still hadn't arranged it yet. There was a small additional bed attached to the room. I left the big bed for Sasson. He asked me to exchange pillows, I should give him the pillow that I hadn't used. "Who knows, is it not possible that you have something infectious?"

"Yes Sasson...one must take precautions, here is the pillow."

I was a little irritated with Sasson. How can he imagine that a cyst is an infectious disease? Later I learned that he was right, that the cyst had actually been inflamed by an infection from an unknown source. He was thinking realistically, not in accordance with *politesse*. His enthusiasm for Arabic literature did not extend to a readiness for getting infected by a disease from an Arab literary figure or for the sake of Arabic literature.

I failed to sleep, and felt I must gather my strength. I didn't want to drive in the dark. It was four o'clock, and clearly I was not going to sleep. It would be a mistake to tarry any further.

"Sasson, let's go."

"Are you able to drive the car now?"

"Yes, the distance is not that far."

I hate to be forced to move when I am ill, indeed illness makes me feel diffident and tense. I was certainly not in a natural condition. I put the car in reverse and felt it bump against something. There was another car next to it that I had not noticed. My car was high off the ground and the other was small and low to the ground. The bump scrapped my driver's side door, but thank God the other car was fine. I had hit its rear bumper. This increased my anxiety. I hate negligent driving and deem it a moral defect. It doubled my pain and anxiety that my condition didn't allow me to search for the owner of the other car to apologize to him. I drove the car from Nazareth to Tel Aviv with all my remaining strength.

"You are another version of Ali Salem...I am now seeing a person for the first time in my life. You have lost your cheerfulness and mirth. You are really a different person."

"I am sick, Sasson. The version you see now is the sick version."

***

In the reception hall of the Ramat Aviv Hotel in Tel Aviv, Sasson said to me: "You drove your car well in any case."

I do not know to this day if he was making fun of me or trying to raise my morale.

"You are now a guest of Tel Aviv University for the period of a week. To be precise, a guest of the Arabic literature department. Lodging includes breakfast only. Any additional expenses will be on your account."

"Thank you Sasson. This is generous of you."

He wrote a note stating that the owner of the car is a guest of Tel Aviv University and then attached it to the car window from the inside. He invited me to dine with him and his wife at a distinguished restaurant outside of the hotel, then returned me back at eight o'clock in the evening. I believe I was disagreeable the entire time. Illness strips us of our identity, it is also a severe form of occupation. I immediately threw myself down on the bed and slept intermittently until morning. It was sleep resembling fainting.

"Ramat Aviv" is both the name of the neighborhood and the name of the hotel which Sasson chose for me. It was near the university and his home, and possessed an important advantage — a spacious interior courtyard shaded by plants and trees where I was able to park my car in peace of mind.

It is difficult to define the character of this suburb or, to be more precise, one should say that it does not reflect the true features of the city of Tel Aviv. Its upper-class neighborhoods are distinguished by cleanliness, quiet and chilliness. But under the best of circumstances they make one feel removed or withdrawn from the city's life. For the life of a city one must look in its old parts.

People walking the street pavement with quick steps, the small cafes and restaurants, the retail stores crammed one up against the other, displaying in their show windows various wares from the refined to the meager, and the old houses with small windows on both sides of narrow alleys which link up the main streets in arching lines, the refreshing sea smell — all these sketch out the distinct human features on the face of a place.

The old houses suffering from neglect, the small alleys, the faint light emanating from the windows and the sounds of enormous buses passing on the streets nearby, the conversation of people, their footfall on the sidewalk, all these make you feel you are moving in a true part of life. But as for the spacious upper-class neighborhoods, with their straight streets and carefully laid out parks, you don't feel they are made by man, but made instead by a director to please the film's stars and the audience, or because the film's script requires it.

***

"Ali...I said to you that lodging includes breakfast only...Do you know about the breakfast here?..There is something called the famous Israeli breakfast...Are you familiar with it?"

"No Professor, unfortunately not. I know only the breakfast famous among intellectuals, which is coffee and cigarettes."

"It is a varied, strong and rich breakfast...You will find everything...It gives you a meal that keeps you from hunger all day."

In truth, the Israeli open buffet breakfast presents you with the equivalent of three meals. If the human body worked like a car engine, that is, gradually drawing down a fuel tank, then it would be possible to have a breakfast that sufficed for a week and not for one day.

I was preoccupied with a question: Why this excess of resources over the breakfast meal among a people known for their austerity? Is it a revival of an ancient tradition?

Many types of breakfasts are well known, the most famous being the

Continental breakfast served by every hotel in the world — jam, butter, tea or coffee, bread. Even the famously rich English breakfast is on the road to extinction, or perhaps is actually extinct. And there is the famous Egyptian breakfast, a plate of *ful*. But there is another breakfast served in my hometown of Damietta about fifty years ago and it is certainly extinct, though I still remember it. Called the "day starter," it was a rich meal served in the early morning, preceding the traditional breakfast by several hours. It consisted of a piece of famous Damietta cheese, a piece of honey pastry or baklava, two eggs fried in country butter, a large cup of tea with milk or, to be more precise, a cup of milk with a bit of tea, then a loaf or half-a-loaf of the type of fine white baguette that no longer exists.

I have no interest in the Continental breakfast, nor in a plate of *ful*. But the Israeli breakfast reminded me of the Damietta day starter. My thoughts summoned up the first time in my life that I heard the word "Jewish." From the storehouse of ancient folk tales residing in the deepest depths of memory, to the surface rose the famous story of the Jew and the Damietta man. Jews have lived in every spot on earth, but Damietta was the only city in which they were unable to live.

And why was that?

In ancient times, a Jew was traveling northward along the Nile riverbank, riding on his donkey in search of a town in which to reside and take up his business, when he arrived at Damietta near the Mediterranean Sea. Before entering the city he saw a man, one of its inhabitants, sitting in the shade of a small hut. He stopped before the man, and descended from the donkey in order to take a short rest. The man welcomed him and asked: "Is there some service I might perform for you?"

So the Jew replied: "Yes. I am in need of dinner...Afterwards dessert...Also I would like some entertainment...and to be kept warm...Likewise I would also like the donkey to eat his dinner...after that I would like a place in which to sleep until morning."

The Damietta man asked him: "What is the budget you have set aside for all this?"

The Jew replied: "Five *milliemes*."

The Damietta man took the five *milliemes* and bought a loaf of bread with one, a *felafel* with one, and a watermelon with the third, and kept the rest. He said: "Your dinner is the bread and *felafel*, and what could be a better dessert than watermelon?"

"What about the entertainment?"

"You will crack open the watermelon seeds...What could be better entertainment?"

"And the heat? I would like to light a fire to warm myself."

"Don't throw away the shells of the watermelon seeds. You can use them as fuel for a fire and warm yourself."

"And the donkey's food?"

"Have you forgotten the watermelon rinds? They are a fine dinner for your donkey."

"And the sleep?"

"Sleep here, sir, in this very place. You are my guest."

So the Jew said to himself: There is no life for me in this city. He mounted his donkey and departed.

In my childhood we understood the tale as accusing the Damietta man of being more stingy than the Jew. But by analyzing its elements I can claim that it does not speak of miserliness or stinginess. It is instead a lesson in avoiding "waste," and how to deal with the elements of life in the most straightened of circumstances without giving up your actual needs for food, sweets, entertainment and warmth. How to consume what you need to stay alive without falling into the sin of squandering resources and energy.

You may say: But the Damietta man tricked the Jew. He was not honest with the Jew, he took five *milliemes* and bought things worth only three.

Incorrect, he was honest. The two remaining *milliemes* were his wage for going to the market and buying the bread, the *felafel,* and the watermelon. They were also his wage for replying to the request for advice...and presenting a realistic feasibility study from the slight budget offered. Thus the Jew bought "know-how."

If I had to invent a new Arabic term borrowed from English, then it would be "the know-how mentality." It is a mentality that deals with life with an all-inclusive understanding, benefiting from all available elements with the minimum amount of waste.

It is not a tight-fisted but rather a selective mentality, it does not ladle from the river of life with a scoop but rather draws from it with a dropper. Likewise, it was natural that drip irrigation technology was invented on one of the kibbutzim and then spread throughout the world.

Then we agree that austerity, avoiding excess and luxury, and minimizing waste to the greatest possible extent are among the prominent traits of the Jewish character. Then why all this luxury and excess in the "Israeli breakfast"? All kinds of cheese, eggs prepared in all the different ways, meats, a type of fish bulging with meat and served lightly salted, jams, honey, yogurt, juices, fruit, fruit compote, all the types of salad that man has invented, and several categories of bread and pastry in addition to several types with names unknown to me...why?

In reviewing what we know from the history of the Jewish people — and I don't claim to be expert in it, I intend here the simple information known to the man in the street — I can say that a collective feeling of insecurity is what fashioned this breakfast.

"It is a new day...You are fortunate to be alive...But no one knows what will happen to you...Eat the food you like best...fill your stomach...Would you like another kind?..take. A second kind?...take. A third, fourth and tenth...The important thing is not to feel that you crave something, that you are forbidden from any food in the coming moment, for no one knows what the next moment will bring."

And what about the Damietti "day starter"?..Is there a collective feeling of insecurity behind it as well?

No...rather the opposite. It reflects a collective feeling of the utmost self-assuredness, peace of mind and entitlement. You are the self-employed owner of a workshop. You awake early to be the first to arrive at work. This splendid "day starter" is your reward, your mark of distinction over the others. You can pay for it since you make more than they as a result of your seriousness and effort. This meal fifty years ago cost about four cents while the regular breakfast did not cost more than one or one-and-a-half cents. Three hours later you will have a regular breakfast, the cooked broad bean and *felafel* sandwich, which you will eat while working. No one will begrudge you or get cross with you...no one will know that you had this early morning meal, no one saw you enjoying the "day starter." The others were all immersed in deep sleep.

***

In the morning, Sasson accompanied me to a reception in a large hall in the university, in which Mrs. Shulamit Aloni, the Minister of Culture and Information, was to meet with writers, literary figures and artists. There I met Abie Nathan, a famous symbol of peace in the region, who mortgaged his restaurant, bought a small airplane and flew it to Egypt before the peace agreement. The Egyptians returned him to Israel where he faced prosecution for taking off from an airport without a license. He also had a ship anchored outside of territorial waters that he turned into a radio station broadcasting programs demanding peace. Then he was sent to prison for violating the Israeli law against having contacts with members of the Palestine Liberation Organization. The first thing that surprises you about Abie Nathan is the brown face overflowing with goodness and tolerance, like the face of the Egyptian peasant from the age before travel abroad. Nothing in his features indicates stubbornness and challenge and the love of adventure.

Shulamit Aloni stood outside the hall and gave a short speech. I noted that none of the ministry's deputies or senior officials were following her wherever she went, it was as if she was just one of the guests. Most likely all the ministry's employees were on vacation that day. I was tired of standing and stepped aside. I sat at one of the plastic tables in the garden outside of the hall, and Shulamit came and sat with me. She didn't talk a lot but listened the whole time. Perhaps the reason for this is that no one in my presence is given the opportunity to talk a lot or even a little, except in rare historic circumstances.

On my way back to the hotel I castigated myself for what I said to Mrs. Shulamit. I regarded it as having transgressed the boundaries of dreams and approached the boundaries of vanity or perhaps exceeded them. I said to her: "Madame...After peace prevails in the region, there is a critical task that awaits you and your colleagues, the ministers of culture and education in the region...There must be new curricula to teach the children that no people is better than the other for any reason...We want them all to learn that there is one God for all...and that all of us belong to one tribe...and...and..."

Shulamit allowed me to talk, then replied tersely: "I'm persuaded."

Only two words, then she looked attentively at my face with a long silent glance as if to ask: But are the others persuaded?

Several days later Mrs. Shulamit asked me to meet her in her office, but unfortunately I had to depart Tel Aviv to continue my excursion. In truth I greatly respect her. She is a statesman in the correct meaning of the word, a serious and courageous intellectual who announces her political views with simplicity and boldness, though they may anger her colleagues and her prime minister.

***

Sasson introduced me to dozens of persons, dozens of names, but my ear is not trained to catch Hebrew names and retain them. One of the persons introduced to me was a Syrian from Aleppo who added: "I will be the first cultural attache in the Embassy of Israel in Damascus."

The declaration surprised me and I didn't comment on it, but my mind began to ponder. He didn't say I would like to be so and so...or I wish to be so and so...rather he said I *will* be. Have the negotiations between Israel and Syria reached the stage that they are choosing personnel for the two embassies? Or are they in Israel working according to the theory of probabilities? Since it is probable that we will shortly reach peace with Syria, okay, so who will be the ambassador and who the cultural attache? Perhaps they informed him in order that he prepare himself and study now.

***

I returned to the hotel almost strangled from the heat, the suit and the necktie pressed on the abscess. The reception clerks all looked up at me with discomforting severity. One woman was closest to a smile, she was beautiful, full-bodied without being obese, and wearing wide eyeglasses that did not hide her features.

"Excuse me, I heard them call you Rahel...What is the correct pronunciation for your name...Is it Rachelle or Rahel?"

"In Arabic it is Rachelle...In the West they pronounce it Rachel and in Hebrew Rahel."

"Okay Rahel...Your name is different in every language...and yet ...there is one thing constant and certain in all languages."

"What?"

"You are quite beautiful."

I said this seriously and severely, so she laughed and all her colleagues smiled. From that moment, they took off the severe mask which they had on their faces whenever they saw me or spoke with me.

***

At eight o'clock in the evening, Farouq Ghoneim came by to see me. He is the number two in the Egyptian Embassy, and he invited Sasson and me to go out. He is about fifty years of age, marked by a high degree of intelligence, enthusiasm and patriotism. These are the traits which characterize the majority of those who work in our diplomatic corps. It's astonishing that the Egyptian bureaucracy raises world-class qualities for export, sending the smartest to the dangerous and sensitive places. As for the idiots, it feeds them to the local market.

He invited us to sit in a magnificent casino on a broad terrace overlooking the streets. We ordered different types of salads. Near to us sat several girls in elegant, modest clothing. After several minutes one of them came to request a light for her cigarette. I lit it for her, then Farouq and I resumed our conversation in Arabic. But did she really "come to request a fire or to light the house on fire?"[13] Several moments later I quickly glanced at her and was surprised to see her take out a lighter from her purse and light a cigarette for her friend. Thus failed the oldest approach known to the Egyptian cinema: Can you give me a light?

At ten o'clock Sasson excused himself and left. He had an appointment at home. I continued talking with Farouq and, when the bill came, glimpsed the amount that he extracted from his pocket. It was about 170 shekels. Oh, the poor guy, about 200 Egyptian pounds for three plates of salad, some sweets and coffee. True, they were rich salads propped up with strange things. But in the end it was salad.

Farouq returned me to the hotel and sat talking with me in the reception hall until one in the morning. It was Thursday, the day after my arrival in Tel Aviv. I confirmed that I would visit them in the Embassy on next Sunday, since Friday and Saturday are the weekend in Israel.

Historic Questions

The ichthyol ointment performed its mission. In the morning I discovered that the abscess had opened. I must see a doctor immediately, I decided. There is no call for negligence since the wound might become contaminated and the matter end in tragedy. Bacteria have become monsters through long contact with human beings. They have become infected, acquiring from man the habit of eating human flesh. They are the only creature that does this.

Reading the work of García Márquez made me terrified of the slightest injury. In one of his short stories, the heroine pricks her finger on a rose thorn in a bouquet of flowers given to her at the beginning of her honeymoon trip. Her finger begins to bleed, and neither she nor her bridegroom are able to stop the bleeding as they travel across Europe on their way to Paris. In Paris, she falls unconscious, they put her in intensive care immediately...and she dies.

***

My appointment with Karen and her husband was at noon. I will ask her to take me to the nearest hospital in Jaffa, I thought, not because I want an Arab physician but because I want a nurse who is dying to treat the author of the play *School of the Trouble-makers*. Indeed I thank God that I am not the author of another play. Would the women physicians and nurses in Nazareth have displayed interest in me had I told them that I wrote *King Lear* or *Hamlet*?

Karen came with her husband, a mild-tempered, constantly smiling person. There was no time to go to Jaffa, since we had an appointment at the writers' union and immediately afterwards a visit to the television station to record a program in English. Okay, I decided, let's go to someplace nearby.

We went to a clinic specializing in emergencies. It appeared to specialize in cases of light emergencies. "What is the fee for an examination?"

"One hundred and forty shekels."

The reader probably expects me either to faint after learning the requested amount or to bargain. I didn't bargain of course. I paid it in surrender, thinking of the amount charged by the greatest Egyptian physicians.

The physician was an elegant youth. His perfect English and his facial features clearly stated that he was a Western Jew, or rather that his Western origin was still fresh. With light touches he circled around the cyst with his fingers. I wanted to break the ice between us so I said: "The touches of your fingers are delicate, doctor."

My intention was to entice him to continue working, but it appears that East is East and West is West as Kipling said. He stopped his work and said: "Your skin is very sensitive."

I took out the prescription written by the doctor in Nazareth and showed it to him. Exactly as I expected, he gave it the look which I know well, the look which precedes the famous sentence: What jerk in God's name prescribed this to you?

But he didn't say it. Instead he said: "This antibiotic has no connection with what you are suffering from."

"How is this? Aren't antibiotics capable of fighting microbes?"

"It is effective in treating only the surface...in killing any bacteria on the skin itself...But what caused the swelling? This doesn't treat the cause. Don't be alarmed, don't think that the swelling was caused by something odious. Look."

He held a piece of paper and a pencil and drew a circle then placed a dot inside of it near the perimeter of the circle. "This is the cause that we don't know." The cause appeared to laugh mockingly now at the antibiotics, knowing that they could not harm it, indeed it was devouring them in enjoyment. "We must know the cause first in order to do away with it."

"And how shall we know the cause?"

"In the laboratory."

"Laboratory?"

"Yes."

"How much will the laboratory cost?"

He replied simply as if he was speaking of a paltry amount: "Oh, about...two hundred shekels."

Oh Lord, it appears that my trip and also my money will be lost between laboratories and physicians. He continued saying: "Isn't it conceivable that the cause is...Leishmania?"

"What is Leishmania, doctor?"

"A parasite...It is precisely the cause of these symptoms."

This was the first time I heard the name of this parasite. Karen also had never heard of it. She promised me to search for it in her medical dictionary.

He prepared a small tube with light yellowish ointment and placed it on the wound. Then he covered it with a gauze bandage. He described the laboratory to Karen and promised that he would be there at eleven o'clock on Sunday morning, the day after next, then he gave me a receipt with the name of the laboratory and information about it.

"Doctor, do you advise me to refrain from using these antibiotics?"

"No...take them."

"Could you please tell me the name of the ointment which you put on me just now?"

He wrote me the name of the ointment, as I requested, since he undertook to do his duty in a complete fashion. But I never sensed for one moment that he took any interest in me. Showing interest is a step higher than merely performing one's job. I didn't feel that emanation of electric current generated by personal interest. It was as if he were eating a frozen meal for breakfast. The distance between us remained very wide. I didn't believe a word he said to me, and it appeared that Karen noticed this.

"Karen, what should we do? Should we meet on Sunday to go to the laboratory?"

"Let's ask Dr. Sasson's opinion. Perhaps he has a better solution."

***

I bought the ointment and several gauze pads and bandages and paid 75 shekels. Then we went to the television station, the English language program, where we would speak together. The program's announcer is a young woman, a student of Karen's, and the television building in Tel Aviv is old and extremely modest. We entered a simple cafeteria, it could have been the cafeteria of the television station in Kafr al-Sheikh. The lady behind the counter was slightly over sixty. There is no sense in saying that she had Arab features since there is nothing on earth called Jewish features or Arab features. They said to her: "So and so...from Egypt."

Her face beamed a wide smile and her eyes brightened with joy. She was an Iraqi Jew.

"I would like coffee *sada*."

"I know what you want...I will serve it the way you like it."

The interview took place in a corner of the courtyard, outdoors under the shade of trees. The announcer introduced Karen and me to the viewers, then started with the question for which I had developed a pat answer: "Why are you here?"

Suddenly she said simply and with a smile: "This morning General Rafael Eitan said that Israel is a foreign body in the region, and it will remain a foreign body in the region forever. What is your view of these words?"

The question surprised me and I was silent for a moment, not because I lacked an answer but because the announcer had thrown me into the mouth of a volcano with a sweet smile. She had drawn me into the center of a political battle between the Labor Party and its rivals. Eitan was clearly responding to Shimon Peres's book, *The New Middle East*.

I admit also to being terrified of Eitan's viewpoint, especially since he is a former chief of staff of the military and former head of intelligence. He said exactly what the worst enemies of peace say of Israel. Am I now — the Egyptian foreigner — to respond to him?

What if I directed at him some strong words, the required thing to do in this situation? In the end, Eitan is a famous Israeli military symbol, and any inappropriate words — or ones considered as such by some — would be refused by all political sides as well as the simple people. Human beings enjoy it when strong words are hurled at their famous political and governmental symbols, but they very much detest it when foreigners get close to these symbols.

I hesitated for several seconds then answered: "The question is...does he want this? Does this make him happy? That Israel is a foreign body in the region and will remain a foreign body? What will he do to prevent Israel from remaining a foreign body in the region? If we assume his words to be true, will the future bring the consequence that Israel will put an end to the region or the region will put an end to it? Or will the conflict circle between the two forever, leaving us in poverty, despair and endless war?..These words don't realize peace in any sense and do not lead to it."

***

Karen returned me to the hotel. At four o'clock in the afternoon Gaby Rosenbaum came to see me and we talked a long while about the Egyptian theater for his doctoral thesis. At five o'clock Sasson came, then at five-thirty a car came from the television station in Jerusalem so that I could attend a live interview there at exactly seven o'clock. Sasson went with me, the trip is about one hour. Approaching Jerusalem, I was overcome with a feeling of tranquility, a feeling I had not felt before. The road ascends into mountains surrounded by green. No one on the face of the earth is capable of describing the road to Jerusalem. If you can imagine an earthly road ascending to paradise, then it must be the road leading to Jerusalem.

Here in fact the three religions must be gathered. The road carries you up among beauty, as if you are in fact on the road to paradise. If the Mu'tazilites[14] used to say: "A thing is forbidden because it is ugly, but not ugly because it is forbidden," then I say: "Jerusalem is holy because it is beautiful, but not beautiful because it is holy."

Only on this road did I understand why people have killed each other for thousands of years for the sake of this place. Now we must have the courage and the will to end this long journey of killing in order that we all enjoy its beauty and holiness. The time has come for Jerusalem to become in word, in deed and by right the City of Peace.

***

I didn't wear a suit, since it would have given me an official appearance that I didn't need. I wore jeans. The director said: "The color of your jacket doesn't go well with the background." So I took it off. Yousef Ismail, the host of the show and a writer as well, spoke about my trip. Once again I was surprised with a question: "We know that most Egyptian intellectuals do not agree with this trip."

I replied: "This is correct, I represent only myself...and there are only a few voices on my side...But I would remind you that the few voices who believe in what they are doing are those that make history."

But why was I surprised by the question?

To be frank, my mind is not trained to do away with compliments on television programs. In front of the camera, we Egyptians are very sweet.

We desist from embarrassment. There is no call to say the truth if it would anger people, and it will anger some of them in every case. For long years I would smile in front of an announcer, who didn't hear a word I said, and carefully select out the abominable. My strongest desire was not to lie, not to be a hypocrite. But the honor of intellect will forever remain speaking the truth, not merely desisting from lies.

I had imagined that my conversation with Yousef would not exceed the circle of welcomes and compliments, but what he meant to say to me was this: Most of your intellectuals do not believe in peace.

It is a dense and trying question, revealing knowledge of my situation. In reply, should I twist and turn in a defense of Egyptian intellectuals that has no creativity or reality? Or should I admit the simple truth? The formulation of the question was highly clever. He didn't accuse the Egyptian intellectuals of not agreeing to peace, so that I would not counter with "Yes, they do want peace and want it on condition a, b, and c...and their viewpoint is d, e, f." But he limited the question to my trip, which most Egyptians intellectuals do oppose. This is correct and I must acknowledge it clearly. "I do not represent the movement of Egyptian intellectuals, I represent myself and a very few voices that have the courage to announce what they think."

***

We returned to Tel Aviv directly after the interview to make a dinner appointment at the home of Farouq Ghoneim at nine o'clock. Lord, what a full day. We passed by Sasson's home to pick up his wife. Among the most pleasant things in life is to be invited to dinner by an Egyptian diplomat, especially when his wife is a gracious lady and talented cook. Farouq whispered in my ear: "Do you need some money? Please, if you need anything at any time, call me immediately...this is my private telephone number at the embassy and here is my home telephone number."

"Dear Farouq...Believe me, I have all that I will need...If I need money at any time I will call on you."

It appears that everything on this trip is really historic, in that it is happening for the first time in history. No one has ever before in my life asked me: Do you want some money?

Millions of questions have been asked of me , but not one of them was this simple, refreshing historic question.

***

The next day we were supposed to go to Haifa to meet the novelists Sami Michael and Emile Habibi, attend a seminar at a kibbutz and then spend the night there. But Sasson had altered the program and preferred that we visit his friend Dr. Markus who would examine me and prescribe the necessary treatment.

Markus is a surgeon who decided on early retirement, in order to devote himself to the one mission dreamed of by all men of reason: enjoying life.

If Shakespeare saw life as a big stage, then certainly Markus sees it as a large restaurant serving barbecued meats. When you see him, fanning with pleasure the grill in his garden, then moving between the grill and the guests, uttering expressions from romantic poetry or classical theater in describing pieces of meat or sausage or the Argentinean spices that he uses, then you might think that Shakespeare was right and that Markus is right as well. What prevents life from being a big stage with a large grill placed on it, with the audience enjoying the meat and Dr. Markus's performance at the same time?

It was a modest villa. We sat in the middle of a large garden along a long table, a number of his friends of both sexes. The clean air in this suburb, the sausage and barbecued meat, and the company of people who love life gave me a feeling of relaxation and a certain amount of delight. It was strange that Markus looked like me, though he was slightly younger and heavier. Sasson had said, correctly, that he would introduce me to an Israeli version of myself.

I approached Markus while he was turning the meat on the barbecue with a surgeon's skill and took a piece of meat immersed in brown sauce. I tasted it and asked: "Is it veal?"

He answered: "Many people think it is veal. In fact it is turkey fed in a special way."

Markus raises poultry and cattle and personally oversees the work on his small farm. Through our conversation I learned that he has a strong tie with Argentina. "What is Leishmania, doctor?"

"You mean lasagna...It is a type of Italian pasta cooked in a certain way to which is added...then you put it in the oven...then..."

"No, Doctor Markus...I mean a parasite."

"Parasite? You mean Leishmania?"

"Yes."

"It exists in plants which grow on the banks of lakes. Yes, it exists in your country."

His answer struck terror into me. Is it possible that this damned Leishmania has infected me?

After I returned to Egypt, I asked my physician friends about this parasite at one of the evenings with Naguib Mahfouz. I learned that it exists in theory only. They had studied it, but knew of no one who had it. A veterinarian told me: "Camels get it, but the references do not note that it afflicts playwrights."

The stomachs of all were full of meat and its accompaniments, everyone became more amiable. These are the pleasurable moments when man enjoys recalling his difficulties. The conversation turned to the new generation and the difficulties with children. "This generation is not responsible. My sister called from Argentina and my son answered. He didn't tell me when I returned. This story was repeated several times, and my sister got angry. Why didn't you tell me my sister called? He answered: She didn't ask me to inform you. She asked me, is so and so there? I said no."

"Imagine, my stepson reprimanded me for speaking on the telephone while driving. Finally he threatened to take the telephone out of the car...Or prevent me from driving the car itself...Imagine, the child instructs me how to drive a car?! And I taught him everything he knows in life...Now he is my guardian."

***

In the living room of the villa, far from the guests, Markus raised the bandage: "No it isn't leishmania...This is a cyst that was infected, became inflamed and turned into an abscess...One moment."

He began to work, I was in pain, but he was talking as if he were dealing with a child. I forgot to tell you that Markus is a pediatric surgeon. "Yes, I know it hurts...But I will finish now...It's nothing...You are not infected with anything...There, I took out all the poison...Now I ask you to wash it off with water."

"Water?"

"Yes, next to the shower. Turn up the water to clean it well."

"In my country they warn us against water entering a wound."

"Clean it with water...Do what I tell you."

My face displayed to him astonishment and lack of trust. We were from two different worlds. He had my features and my love of life, and my same esteem for barbecued meat. However, we differed now, one didn't trust the other.

All the misfortunes of man begin at this point. My lack of trust in his words called into question his competency as a doctor. He wanted politely to direct my attention to the fact that as a physician he is responsible for what he says. He said: "Our teachers, who are among the greatest surgeons, taught us that the best way to cleanse a wound is to use water."

That is actually what happened. I cleaned the wound with water, dried it, and put on a small medical band-aid. I was certain that I was on the way to recovery and that Markus had treated me correctly, not because he is a good physician but because I believe and trust in those who love life and not in those who claim that they understand it.

In the University

A meeting with professors and graduate students of Arabic literature and drama at Tel Aviv University. The weather was hot, I felt almost strangled inside the suit and tie. Sasson introduced me to the audience with a concise statement, then grabbed a book in English, opened it to a certain page and gave it to one of the students.

"This is a book written by Dr. Mustafa Badawi from Oxford University on Arabic literature. Let us hear now what he wrote about Ali Salem."

The youth read the page to the audience. Strangely enough, five years earlier, Dr. Trevor LeGassick, professor of Arabic literature at the University of Michigan, cited the same reference when he introduced me to the professors at the university.

I was gripped with the feeling that Sasson wanted to say to the audience: Don't think that we are giving this man a place he doesn't actually deserve merely because he came to Israel. Listen what a professor of Arabic literature at Oxford University says about him.

***

I said to them: "Gentlemen, in spite of the extreme heat, I wore a suit to express my respect for you and for this occasion. And to prove to you that I owned a suit...But now I want to be myself and to sit with you in comfort."

I took off my jacket and tie and rolled up my shirt sleeves, at which they burst into laughter and applause. There was a question asked of me at two separate meetings: "Is a writer of yours able to live off his writings?" "Yes...a high percentage of our writers live from their writings and I am one of them."

If asked the question here in Egypt, I would give a much longer answer. I would probably answer: The writer is able to live with difficulty or can scrape by from writing, but he is only able to live a comfortable life when he refrains from writing or is unable to do so. It depends on the definition of writing. When you read the wealthy writers of Egypt, you will discover that they have created a new type of writing. It is possible to give it the name "un-writing," for it is "diet" writing devoid of calories.

Another question: "Are there personal ties between your rulers and your literary figures?"

I answered: "I don't believe there exists on earth friendly ties between the ruling power and literary figures. I know that Shimon Peres says sometimes, 'I called my friend the writer Amos Oz and he said to me this and that...'" Everyone laughed, it seems that Peres uses this sentence a lot.

Peres is a special case among rulers and politicians. He is a literary man who lost his way and became a statesman, or perhaps he lives in a free zone on the borders between the state and literature. But in general I do not imagine a friendly tie between men of power and men of letters. The relationship between them is wary and closer to hate. Especially for the playwright, it is a relationship of conflict usually ending in silencing of the latter, or in sending him into exile or imprisoning him. This has happened to many throughout the world. The only time in history that a playwright emerged from prison to become a statesman was Vladislav Havel in Czechoslovakia.

This is the exception that proves the rule. There is a great deal of envy between the politician and the creator. "You write something and people take money out of their pockets to read or see it. People go out to theaters and pay money to hear what you say...Whereas I do the impossible in order to find people to listen to me."

I ate lunch at the faculty club. In all large universities there are magnificent restaurants that serve food that isn't so magnificent. I prefer the students' cafeteria, closer to my heart and stomach.

***

"Rahel my dear, I am traveling next Monday to Beer Sheva. They will send a car for me here at the hotel. Is it possible to leave my car at the hotel for these two days?"

"With pleasure."

Sasson feared that the hotel would refuse to allow the car to remain in the courtyard while I was gone. He intended to speak with the university officials about the university garage, but I reassured him. He said: "They clearly like you at the hotel. But does Rahel have the authority to take decisions there?"

I answered: "History proves that beautiful women wherever they are, in hotels or in governments, have the authority to take decisions."

***

"Hello...I'm Oz Miller, a poet and symphony conductor in Tel Aviv."
"Nice to meet you."
"May I meet with you?"
"Please."

He came to the hotel, a beautiful child about sixty years old, speaking English slowly and clearly: "When President Sadat visited Jerusalem, I wrote a poem and sent it to him. He answered me with this personal letter..."

"I would like to conduct the Cairo Symphony Orchestra...and that you should send a Cairo conductor to conduct the Tel Aviv Symphony in exchange...This is my hope and the dream of my life."

He spoke in the low voice of a supplicant, as if reciting a prayer. I felt pained. How to explain to him?

"My dear Oz....Believe me, I am just an Egyptian artist. I don't possess influence of any kind. But I have friends in the Ministry of Culture. I will inform them of your desire."

"What are the obstacles that would prevent this?"

"There are many obstacles that are difficult to explain to you. This step can only be achieved in the framework of a complete cultural plan, aiming to transform the theoretical peace between the two countries into a tangible reality on the ground that is experienced by both peoples. And through it, peace will take on a true meaning. But this takes time."

Of course I spoke a language that he didn't understand...nor did I.

"But President Sadat wrote me this personal letter...read it."

The letter is a splendid literary piece in English. Clearly the writer in Sadat's office was aware that he was replying to a poet. I wonder who he is.

"Yes, Oz...But Sadat died...And with him died many things."

"What should I do?"

"Don't despair of trying. You are asking a noble and simple thing. It must happen...When?...Believe me, I don't know."

And Oz left.

I imagine Oz now sitting in his room writing the opening verses of a poem. I want to understand...We signed a peace agreement with the Egyptians many years ago...And I want to go safely to Cairo, to conduct its orchestra in peace...*Ya Salam*, oh peace, oh dear.

Then they send a maestro safely to conduct the Tel Aviv Symphony in peace.. *Ya Salam*, oh dear.

Then he returns safely to Cairo...Why doesn't this happen, oh God?

***

An interview with *Haaretz*, the most prestigious daily newspaper. They sent me a photographer one hour before the interview. He said: "Pardon me, I am a professional photographer and thus will need some time."

He was indeed a professional photographer. He knew that a person is not always himself and that it takes a while to catch the right moment. One must arrive at the picture that expresses your truth.

He is of Lebanese extraction: "My father and mother spoke Arabic, but unfortunately I don't. This angers me and holds me back...I feel I am working with one arm."

His words rang in my ears. His inability in Arabic holds him back and makes him feel as if he is working with one arm. He is a proficient professional, but he lacks one arm which is the Arabic language. When he masters it he will work with two arms, in a natural way and with all his energy, and he will be more professional and more talented. Is this not the situation of Israel?

But I have not discovered a new truth. The great Israeli poet Amichai discovered it when he wrote: "It is not time which distances me from my childhood, but this city, and everything in it. Now we ought to learn Arabic."

Amichai made a big step on the road to peace when he asked his people to learn Arabic. I also ask those who want to have a role in the future of Egypt and the region to learn Hebrew. It is a wide entrance onto the road of peace. It is a difficult task for my generation. Hatred and wars have not left space in our minds to learn it.

My words might seem strange now, in the shadow of hatred fed by the capitals of the desert and the prophets of fascism. But when peace prevails in the region, and freedom is victorious and individual human rights are achieved, then people will look back in wonder and disgust at what we did to each other. The time will come when the residents of the region, like other respectable creatures of God living elsewhere, believe that there is nothing more holy on earth than human life. All the "noble" ideas that have led to killing people, to terrifying and impoverishing them and turning them into victims roaming the desert, begging a morsel of bread and a drink of water...these are nothing other than crimes in the record of the region's history, and the possessors of these ideas are mere criminals.

There is nothing on the face of the earth more holy than political and economic freedom and individual human rights. Anything that prevents or hinders or holds them back is nothing other than a crime.

The Road to Beer Sheva

"The invitation to spend two nights in Beer Sheva is from Abdallah Rabi'a."

"Who is he, professor?"

"I think he works in the Beer Sheva municipality. He's a friend of the novelist Sami Michael."

The drive from Tel Aviv to Beer Sheva takes less than two hours. A little before Beer Sheva, the driver told me: "Now we are approaching Faluja. I will show you the place where Nasser was surrounded."

The car stopped near a field.

I went back in time. This place has affected my life and the lives of millions of human beings. Here in 1949 Nasser was surrounded, together with thousands of Egyptian troops. Field negotiations took place here in a tent between him and his group of Egyptian colleagues and Israeli officers. This is a natural affair that often occurs on the field of battle. There is an important sentence in the memoirs of one of the Israeli officers, Yigael Yadin: "In these meetings, these young men realized that their battle was not here." Indeed, in his book *Philosophy of the Revolution*, Nasser wrote: "There we realized that our real battle was in Cairo."

And so it was. After the tanks returned from Faluja to their bunkers in the fields of the Abbasiyya district of Cairo, they rested some time from the fatigue of the road, then went out into the streets of Cairo to undertake their real battle. Since that time, all the residents of the region have lived in a state of mental war.

A number of military officers in other Arab capitals made the same astonishing discovery — that their real battle was in their capitals. So they also took their tanks into the streets and eliminated the civilian version of government that was blocking their path to the liberation of Jerusalem. They then eliminated, quickly or gradually, human rights in their countries. But we would slight them if we didn't also admit that they succeeded in adding several hundred thousand to the number of refugees, just as they added hundreds of thousands to the list of fatalities, the wounded and maimed. They naturally didn't forget to swell the ranks of widows, bereaved parents and orphans.

We should also concede that these military rulers succeeded in relieving the Arab nation of the burden of governing a great deal of real estate, without forgetting to ensure for its inhabitants the greatest amount of misery, suffering, loss, imprisonment, detention, killing, torture, the breaking of bones and...the greatest amount of pounding that a people has known in this age of human rights, greater even than what these rulers themselves were able to provide to their peoples.

Later, some thought that the road to Jerusalem lay through Amman. It took the slaughter of several thousand Palestinians on a black day in September to prove that this idea was mistaken.

Others supposed that the road to Jerusalem passed through Kuwait. All the Arab road and bridge experts failed to convince them that this notion was mistaken. The West had to come with its means of persuasion to prove that Jerusalem was actually very far from Kuwait. The joke told in Israel was that the Iraqi regime was the first Arab regime to undertake true "normalization" with Israel, since all of the rockets that it fired at Israel fell on areas inhabited by Iraqi Jews.

Our losses were trivial, several hundred thousand casualties and several hundred billion dollars. An entire people lives behind the walls of a republic of fear in conditions that not even Hell itself is able to match.

"All this is a mistake, " you say. "Jerusalem will be liberated when we march towards it directly on the highway, in an armored vehicle named Arab unity...When the Arab countries are united, we will advance on and reclaim Jerusalem...or rather all of Palestine."

There go the tanks into the desert, headed south this time, towards Aden to destroy the enemies of Arab unity.[15] But it turns out that the enemies of Arab unity, as defined by the authorities, are human beings...public utilities...buildings...homes...water pumping stations...oil refineries...The true enemy of unity is life...Life must be destroyed to save unity!

Indeed it is a mental state of war.

This is a state that envelopes the mind and has no connection to actual war on the ground. It's different from combat. In combat, generals plan seriously and realistically without illusions in order to achieve a victory sufficient to create peace. But in a mental state of war you fight without going into the field, you are transformed into a cannon without ammunition, a smoke bomb, a pop gun. All your actions and words are transformed into slogans and battle cries. It is a state of hatred of self and of others; it is the highest degree of lie.

In a mental state of war, you're prepared to give up all your human rights, and this is the worst part of it. In order to convince you that it is an actual war, others will put you in a narrow trench and turn off the lights, leaving you in pitch darkness. Then they play a tape of sound effects on giant loudspeakers. All the sounds of war are recorded on the tape. You actually feel the shells raining down on the trench, and so you try not to budge out of fear of getting hit. After some time passes — I mean your present and future — you will consider yourself lucky because you haven't yet died.

Even when they stop the tape to replace it with another, and there are a few moments of silence, they say to you: "These are the most dangerous moments of battle! The enemy is silent because he is planning...Don't think you are safe!..These are the moments when the enemy is conniving with international imperialism and planning to put an end to you...Be on guard...Be on guard against getting out of the trench...They are planning now to transform you from an Arab into a Middle Easterner."

At this you cower inside the trench and you are overcome with terror at the prospect of being turned into a Middle Easterner.

Of course you don't ask: What's the meaning of the Middle Eastern market? Is it like the Friday farmers market? What are its advantages for me? What are its disadvantages? What does it mean that Israel will have hegemony over this market? How can I prevent this hegemony? The word "hegemony" itself...what does it mean?

You won't ask questions for a simple reason. In a state of war, no one argues...or ask questions. "Is this the right time man?...Get back to the trench immediately."

The mental state of war can be comfortable, indeed pleasurable, especially in the absence of critical thinking, since it arises directly from the most basic of instincts: hostility.

Thus said a friend named Hilmi, a retired police officer and an intellectual. He was working as the director of security in the New Valley province.[16] This province has not had any thieves. The only theft in the province happened on his watch. His apartment was broken into, and robbed by the policeman who was assigned to guard him. I cite this incident to illustrate the danger of being an intellectual and a director of security at the same time. Your learning gives you an amount of ethics that others interpret as weakness...This is the attitude towards intellectuals among rulers and among thieves as well.

Hilmi said to me: At that time in 1948 I was a student at Benha secondary school. We went by train to Cairo, several hundred of us, and joined a crowd of thousands in the Opera Square. The leaders stood on a balcony of the old Shepheard's Hotel and addressed us...Hasan al-Banna, Ahmad Hussein, Fathy Radwan, Abdallah Pasha Lamloum, and others whose names I can't recall.[17]

Hasan al-Banna said: "The problem is one of weaponry. If we need weapons, let's take them from our enemies and throw them into the sea."

Ahmad Hussein said: "I am going to the field of battle in Palestine carrying my rifle on my shoulder, and he who wants to follow will have God's reward."

Of course he didn't go to Palestine. Leaders are generally too clever to go to battlefields.

As for Abdallah Pasha Lamloum, who was wearing traditional bedouin dress, he pulled out a revolver, shot a bullet into space and shouted: "This is the first shot. I fire it for you, Oh Palestine."

The crowd went wild. They returned him to the balcony after several minutes to fire off another shot, as if he were a singer responding to the request for an encore.

From that moment, the battle cries exploded. Perhaps the most important was: "The sword has spoken — so be silent, oh pen."

I believe this scene summarizes clearly the basic features of the mental state of war. Lamloum Pasha fired off a shot into the air for the sake of Palestine, and to increase the ecstasy they demanded another round. Since then rounds into the air have followed one after another in every Arab capital, over microphones, newspapers pages and cameras.

Since that moment the sound effects tape has been playing.

As for the slogan which asks the sword to speak and the pen to be silent, it was impossible to achieve the first part. As is well known, swords don't speak. So it sufficed for the Arab nation to realize the easier and more beneficial part about silencing the pen.

Question: Is it possible to transform the mental state of war into actual war?

The answer: Yes...when people overdose on it, intending to reach a higher degree of ecstasy resulting from the absence of consciousness. Put a large quantity of weapons and ammunition in a bag, add a certain amount of lies and illusions, throw in a number of irresponsible men, seal the bag and leave it in an open place among human beings. Definitely it will blow up in their midst, after several months or years.

Only once did the bag blow up without killing anyone. It happened during the split-up of the Egyptian–Syrian United Arab Republic, for reasons extraneous to the wishes of the parties concerned. Fortunately for the two peoples, there is no common border between Syria and Egypt.

The true and legitimate war is a defensive war, when war is the only option. In 1956 and in 1973 we had to fight, it was the only option both times. Twice the Egyptians undertook a true war that had nothing to do with mental deterioration. Compare the 1956 song "God is Great" with the 1967 tune "Don't worry, Oh President, About the Americans, Oh President." Listen to the words of the latter song: "Around you are the bravest of men, gunfire opens the way with fire into the hearts of man...It is only a tussle between the President and America...why would we die in it?"

Compare that with the song of Baligh Hamdy in 1973, "I on the Folk Violin will Sing." The October 1973 War was a true defensive war, led by professionals. It happened on the ground and wasn't a state of hysteria turning the mind into a piece of mud.

Before traveling to Israel, I spoke with many friends who opposed my trip. I listened carefully to all they said. I feared I was missing some angle or key element that would lead to my harming the interests of the Egyptian people. But all I heard were excuses, all arising from a mental state of war, from hatred. The only difference between them and me is that I want to get rid of this hatred. I decided to participate in the creation of peace.

Peace is also a mental state. I must compel my mind and the minds of others to enter this state. I have great faith that this will be easy for those who seek freedom.

"Dear driver, I have surely seen enough of Faluja. Permit us to continue on the way to Beer Sheva...We've tarried here too long."

The Strike Leader

Strikes are a phenomenon common to societies that embrace political and economic freedom. A group of human beings decides to stop working, to gather and present their demands to those capable of resolving them. Previously they had issued their demands and met with officials, but had received no response. Perhaps they had received a response perceived as not resolving their demands.

A strike aims through pressure to reach the point at which negotiations with the employer become necessary. By abstaining from work, the strikers put the fingers of the managers between their teeth and slowly bite down on them. And the managers do the same thing to the strikers until one of the parties screams: ouch!

All types of regimes in all political systems naturally abhor strikes, while the people deem them desirable. Those who think that man loves work and accepts it voluntarily are mistaken. We are in any case compelled to work.

Strikes of course hamper the interests of large sectors of the society, but they're a price for democracy. They raise the society's body temperature, indicating that there is damage to a part which requires immediate treatment. The body of the society rids itself of the poison that was formed inside its layers and continues on its way, stronger and healthier.

Strikes have rules — no fanaticism, no convulsions, no losses, nor destruction of property. Be careful not to antagonize public opinion, or to affect the public interest in a way that turns it against you, causing you to lose the issue and your demands.

Societies that do not embrace political and economic freedom do not know strikes for a simple reason. The people in these societies do not work and thus how can they abstain from doing something that they do not do in the first place?

The only possible form of strike in these societies is for people to work and by so doing to put the government officials in an embarrassing situation, compelling them to issue more laws and decrees which guarantee that they won't work. Only government officials are allowed to have open-ended, unlimited strikes. From here begins the bargaining: "Please work...Oh Lord, work...This is terrible...Our interests are being damaged."

"Right away...here we go...We will get to work, yes sir...Okay, by God, we're going to work."

"When?"

"Hey everybody take it easy...How can a person work straight away just like that? Don't we need to study first and learn the correct techiques for work? And in which direction? And with what criteria? Aren't there rules governing work?"

"All right, why don't you work like the others?"

"Which others? China or America? England? Sudan or Libya? France? Or Italy?

"Enough... Work like America."

"Do we have the capacities of the Americans?"

"Then like China."

"No way. The Chinese heritage is different from our heritage."

"Can you work like England or France?"

"Of course not. The English speak English and the French French. How can we work like them?"

"Then why not work like people who have succeeded?"

"Oh man, what do you think we are doing?...This is exactly what we are doing...But take it easy a little."

"All right."

Thus the strike continues.

***

In every strike one person, or sometimes several people, becomes the strike leader or leaders. This person is in the best of spirits when creating a strike. Such was the student who entered our class calmly some forty years ago. When the teacher turned to him to ask why he was there, he suddenly shouted: "Teaching is forbidden today...Long live the student union!"

We would leave the classroom immediately. How sweet and refreshing were those moments when we learned that school was off on exactly that day!

As a youth I participated in many strikes and demonstrations, but I fail to recall what they were for or against. I remember only the feeling of ecstasy when we left the classrooms to gather in the large courtyard of the school and listen to the strike speeches. We cheered loudly after finding a legitimate justification for abstaining from studying. The commandment was clear and unambiguous. Today school is forbidden. Who here would brave the forbidden?

Abdallah Rabi'a, a former social researcher and presently a senior official in the union of researchers, statisticians and sociologists, is a strike leader.

A Jew of Iraqi origin, he retired several years ago. Time has not harmed this large man's handsome features or jovial spirit, perhaps because he continues to pursue his passion for strikes. Organizing strikes since a young man in Baghdad has preserved his youthfulness.

He was waiting for me in the hotel (the Desert Inn) with two young social researchers, Majid and Ishaq, both of bedouin origin.

Abdallah spoke to me passionately of the strike he was currently organizing. The social researchers were demanding an increase in pay. Prior to military rule in Iraq, the stupid despotic governments there allowed people not only to strike and demonstrate, but also to shout opposition slogans. Abdallah didn't mention the name of the political faction to which he had belonged, it wasn't important and I didn't ask him. What was important was that it allowed him to pursue his art as a strike leader.

"A leader of the cell in the party in Iraq summoned me and said: 'Abdallah, you are responsible for the wounded and injured in tomorrow's demonstration. We will clash with the police and provoke them to hit us. Some will be injured of course. Prepare the necessary provisions.'"

So Abdallah bought a large quantity of gauze, cotton, mercurochrome and iodine. When the demonstration ended, the party official summoned him and said angrily: "Are you pleased Abdallah?...No one was injured."

Abdallah replied: "What do you want me to do? Should I hit them for you myself?"

I wonder what were the chants that Abdallah was leading? What were the slogans that he stayed up all night writing on cloth banners? "Palestine is Arab...Down with Zionism."

On that day, or to be more precise, during that demonstration, he cleared his throat in preparation for the famous chant, "Down with Zionism," when he was stunned by another chant, which started behind him, as if it were the shout of fate: "Death to the Jews."

That cry in Baghdad was not in jest, it was meant literally.

At that moment of *gestalt*, Abdallah discovered that Abdallah Rabi'a the Iraqi Arab from Baghdad and Abdallah Rabi'a the Jew were one and the same. Whereas death was not demanded for Abdallah the Arab it was demanded for Abdallah the Jew. So he moved to Israel.

***

"It is known that you are against Zionism."
"I was against it...Now I am here."
"Why?"
"I came fearing for my life."
"Your name is Abdallah...Isn't it?"
"Yes."
"Okay...Now your name is Ovadiah"
"Why? My name is Abdallah."
"Abdallah is the same as Ovadiah...and Rabi'a is Rabi...Your name now is Ovadiah Rabi."

Today he is Ovadiah Rabi, though he was able to keep his old first name, at least among his friends, and became known as Abdallah Ovadiah. He had been one servant of God but became two in two different languages.[18] They deprived him of the name he was raised on but, praise God, they permitted him to pursue his fine art, strikes and demonstrations. Who would permit him this anywhere else in the whole Middle East?

***

We ate dinner in an Argentinean restaurant. (Where are you, Doctor Markus, to show them how to barbecue and to show them also the quantity that should be served?) Majid and Ishaq were with us. Abdallah asked me to go to bed early since we would travel to Eilat at six in the morning. "I'll ask the hotel to wake you at five-thirty...We'll return the same day."

"There's a problem, Abdallah. I can't open my eyes in the morning before drinking coffee. Hotel restaurants usually don't open their doors before seven in the morning." The problem was solved immediately. I took a thermos filled with coffee when I went upstairs to my room. In the morning I returned it to the reception desk.

The road from Beer Sheva to Eilat was long, about 240 kilometers, through the Negev Desert. We ate breakfast after about an hour in a cafeteria on the road. Despite the continuous signs of urbanization, the Negev Desert is keen to remind you the entire time that it is a desert.

About thirty kilometers from Eilat the driver said a few words in Hebrew to Abdallah. I gave Abdallah a questioning look and he answered me: "He says this is a tourist area...King Solomon mined copper here...Do you want to see it?"

Abdallah said it without enthusiasm, as if he were suggesting that we continue on our way, so I corrected him: "King Solomon mined copper here? No, Abdallah...It was the ancient Egyptians who mined copper here." Abdallah laughed a lot, but I continued in a serious vein: "Abdallah, the ancient Egyptians extracted gold and copper from southern Sinai..Look around you, Abdallah...The mountains and hills here are the same as in southern Sinai...An extension of them. I feel as if I am driving in southern Sinai. Let's go take a look, Abdallah."

The driver doubled back a little then took a right into a passage between the mountains. At the end of the passage there was a gate and near it a kiosk in which stood an employee. We bought tickets and drove in. Abdallah exchanged a few words with the employee then turned to me: "I informed him that you are Egyptian and he said that there is a film on the area in Arabic in twenty minutes."

In the large courtyard in the midst of the mountains stood a simple building, merely one room resembling a garage. Inside was an auditorium with stone benches and a large television system.

Two tourist buses came with a large group of students from the Upper Galilee. We sat on the stone benches and the film on the area began. The place is named Timna Mountain. The narrator began speaking and the film reviewed the features of the place. My expectations were correct. The narrator said: "Here the ancient Egyptians mined raw copper." Then scenes of a temple with Egyptian inscriptions, then the slag and refuse that indicates the methods by which the Egyptians extracted copper from the mines.

After viewing the film we continued on the road to Eilat. We didn't have time to visit the area's ruins and it sufficed to see the film. I began to speak seriously while Abdallah roared with laughter. "Oh Abdallah, there is no need to speak about historical rights. You saw for yourself...We Egyptians were here thousands of years ago...No need for one of us to say to the other: 'We were here thousands of years ago.' Saying this doesn't get us anywhere. We must say: 'I am here now, and you are here now, and we must find a way to live together in peace.'

"Here and now Abdallah, here and now. I don't believe all that History says, especially when it calls me to slaughter you, or pushes you to kill me. I only believe those parts that push me to live with you in peace...Of how many moments is history composed, Abdallah? Billions of billions, isn't it so? Why chose those moments that enjoin all of us to put an end to the other? Why not chose other moments through which we can achieve peace?

"Why don't we take advantage of this moment in which I am sitting with you now in a car? It's also an historical moment. I believe it's historical because it is a moment in which History discovers that it was mistaken. Okay, come now let's think differently about Timna Mountain. Let's assume we are holding here a distant moment of time residing deep in the hollows of History, and over here we are holding the present moment in which we are living. If we draw a straight line between the two, what's the result?

"The result is that the area of Timna Mountain belongs to the Egyptians. Our right to it is clear. We didn't make the film. It is a frank admission of yours to our historical right to this place. Thus we will demand the extension of the Egyptian border thirty kilometers to the north of Eilat. The Egyptian temple here wasn't obliterated or destroyed. It exists, complete with inscriptions. The matter only requires a letter of one page to the UN Security Council attaching a copy of the film. We will ask the entire world to answer this question: Were the Egyptians here or not? They will answer yes, they were here. So Timna Mountain is ours by historical right.

"What will you say to the people of the world? Will you say that the ancient Egyptians are not the Egyptians of today? That the ancient Pharaohs came from a distant planet then went away? No one would believe you. Don't be frightened Abdallah, believe me we will not demand of you Timna Mountain, despite the fact that the name is beautiful and useful for rhyming anthems, songs and chants. The issue, Abdallah, is what will we do here and now. What will we do to live in freedom and peace, to plant the desert that we both have?

"But I propose to speak of a subject close to your heart, Abdallah. Assume that we in Egypt are leading a big demonstration to inflame the masses and put them in a mental state to demand the return of Timna

Mountain. What would be the slogans and songs and speeches? What do you think of this song: 'My beloved, with sword and shield, is out in the Timna battlefield' or 'Forget all other sites, for Mount Timna we must fight' or 'We must stick to the truth, to Timna Mountain, oh youth!'

"No, Abdallah, not hot enough to inflame the masses? You want something hotter? 'Weep, shed tears like a fountain, gone from us is Timna Mountain.' Or: 'The troops all shout hurrah when they win back Mount Timna.' 'Those who trade and those who bargain, give us back Timna Mountain.' Some of the slogans must be frivolous. Nonsensical. The people love this type a lot. For example, 'Shine, shine, oh sword' or 'Burn, burn, oh candle' etc."

Abdallah laughed with pleasure and his eyes brightened like a child's, as if he imagined himself leading this demonstration.

Here and now, Abdallah, what shall we do here and now?

***

I didn't like Eilat and I don't like cities built for tourism. Their builders strive to make everything pretty and shining, and this is not the nature of life. The driver took us to Taba, which is several minutes distant from Eilat. Abdallah asked if we could cross the border into Egypt. I refused, I have a single entry visa to Israel. What would happen if they didn't permit me to re-enter while my car is in Tel Aviv?

We returned to Beer Sheva...We stopped several times to have a coffee on the road. One of the restaurants was built of bamboo, timber and tree trunks. Abdallah said: "I know the owner of this restaurant. He was a paratrooper. He undertook several operations in the war and later was considered a hero. One night he crossed the border into Jordan without orders and killed some soldiers there, so they expelled him from the army."

This is a disaster. Killing sometimes makes some people heroes and peace terrifies them. It simply means they take off the raiment of heroism and become normal people.

A rooster roaming the place caught my eye. He was unbelievably large. What did they do so to make the rooster reach that size? Is it hormones? Why? I began to contemplate the thick plumage that covered his eyes and beak and was creeping over his talons. He certainly would not be good to eat after his meat became like wood. No need to search for distant reasons; this rooster became this size because no one slaughtered him.

***

We returned to the hotel in Beer Sheva about one hour after sunset. Abdallah said: "You know that tomorrow I am very busy preparing a strike. I will go to sleep now. At five in the morning the driver will take me to Tel Aviv, I have a breakfast appointment at seven with a senior official about the strike. Then the driver will return to Beer Sheva to take a nap. He will come for you at two in the afternoon, to take you to Tel Aviv and then take me to Jerusalem where I have a task to do. At ten in the morning Majid and Ishaq will come to show you around Beer Sheva, then you will return safely to Tel Aviv. Bring your wife next time. My wife would very much like for you two to visit us."

***

"This is a rehabilitation center for the war wounded."

"No Majid...Sorry Ishaq. I will not visit this place. I don't need to see because I know well what war does to people." I hate this gruesome custom which reeks of hypocrisy, the custom of visiting war victims as if they were a tourist attraction. I shudder when I see a notable personality visiting war wounded on television, carrying roses and presents and smiling at them while the cameras roll remorselessly and stupidly. What can he do for them other than look at them? Nothing.

I have seen enough of this in my country. I live near a rehabilitation center. I have also read enough of wounded war heroes whom people support after the war has ended. Tell me honestly: What reward or recompense could all the people in the world present to this youth after a missile took away his eyesight or crippled his movement?

God, if I had something to give to these youths of ours and yours, then I would have given it immediately. "My friends, I thank you both for your concern for me and your generosity. Please convey to Abdallah Ovadiah my deepest thanks. Now please take me back to the hotel since it is nearly two o'clock when the car will take me back to Tel Aviv."

***

"Rahel, Praise the Lord. I was gone for two nights and returned to find my bags in their place, my car in its place and you behind the reception desk. And the most amazing thing is that you are still so beautiful. Do I have any messages?"

"Yes, Mr. Farouq Ghoneim from the Egyptian Embassy asked you to confirm your attendance at a dinner at his home on Friday evening."

"Okay...let's see. My stay here on the university's account ends on Friday morning."

"Yes."

"But I will leave Saturday morning in order to attend this dinner. This additional evening will be on my account. Would you please — my sweet — look into the necessary discount for me?"

Hotels in Israel exempt you from paying a 17 percent tax when you pay in dollars. But I desired more of course. Rahel sat at the computer and began to work, She remained working such a long time on her calculations that it appeared that she was squeezing the computer. Finally she said: "56 dollars."

"Ah. Is this all that is possible?"

"Yes...We charge the university 85 dollars."

"I thank you Rahel. By the way, you are the first five-star person working in a three-star hotel."

***

Attending the party at Farouq's home was a large group from the Israeli Foreign Ministry in addition to several academic personalities from the Peace Now Movement and a big surgeon who had been a prisoner in the 1973 War and had performed surgery on a number of Egyptian soldiers.

Farouq and his wife were excellent hosts. An atmosphere of warmth and friendliness prevailed. One of the guests asked me: "Can you summarize for us in one sentence how you were treated here?"

"The Ashkenazis respected me, the Sephardis loved me."

"Can you explain?"

"The Jews of Western origin treated me with respect and politeness while the Jews of Eastern origin treated me with love and joy. By the way, I had to come here to discover the error in this appellation. They are actually Arab Jews, and this puts more burden on us Egyptians."

"How is that?"

"Wait for my book."

The guests departed while I sat speaking with Farouq. He turned on the television. The announcer was talking with a person wearing a uniform, clearly an important person in the police. He was answering questions in a low voice and appeared to be afraid to look into the camera. I noticed that Farouq was smiling.

"Who is he?"

"The head of the police."

"What is he saying?"

"'I didn't commit any offense. I didn't contravene any law or regulation. I behaved like any ordinary citizen, without connection to my position.'"

"What's his story?"

"He obtained a discount of forty percent from one of the hotels and is compelled to resign. It is the right of any citizen to request as a matter of courtesy the same discount or better from any hotel. But why did the head of the police get it? What will he pay in return? The press pursued him after the hotel published his picture with some hotel guests in the swimming pool. The press considered this an advertisement, meaning that he obtained a discount in exchange for this advertisement."

"Are you sure that he obtained only a discount and not the hotel itself?"

"Yes."

"What a miserable wretch. He got a forty-percent discount at the hotel and the press is forcing him to resign? Praise the lord, Rahel gave me about the same discount, and no one will force me to resign or even to work."

***

Corruption does not shake the ancient state. Its strong, well-rooted pillars, formed over thousands of years, are capable of supporting its structure whatever the extent of the rot which eats away at them. It employs timeless techniques and possesses the power, when exposed to sudden danger, to rid itself of corruption.

Every state possesses a margin of administrative and political corruption, wider or narrower but always present. It appears that people here are frightened of corruption for practical and not moral reasons. People are the same everywhere and there is nothing which leads one to believe that some are more moral than others.

Here they are aware that tolerating corruption in political and government circles, whatever its size, guarantees the end of the state, since they are still in the first stages of state formation. I will be bold and say: They are still in the nursery of history, and thus treat their statesmen severely. At the uncovering of the first mistake, their statesmen pay a higher price than any other citizen.

At this point, after a few days of quick visits to certain places, it is possible to view Israel as a multi-national stock company with a tightly run accounting department. This department strives to distribute end-of-year profits in a strict way to its shareholders. No shareholder gets preferential treatment over the other shareholders. Other departments are extremely important, for example the department of obtaining money from outside, but all departments and committees are subordinate to the accounting department which represents the highest place in the building of Israel, above it is only heaven. No one is above the accounting.

"You want to work in the state? In politics? You want to pursue public service? Good, welcome...The only requirement, kind sir, is that you agree that we will turn on upon you and your work a thousand projectors, the biggest one is named the press. We the press are talking with you now. Answer us. What is your name and work?"

"My name is Yitzhak Rabin. I am the leader of the Labor Party and the Prime Minister."

"You violated the law Mr. Rabin...Your wife has an account in a non-Israeli bank."

"I didn't violate the law. This is a very old subject. I was the Israeli ambassador in America. According to the law, we had to open an account in an American bank."[19]

"Why didn't you close the account when you completed your residence there?"

"It was a trivial amount...about $1,500 and we forgot it."

"Oh no, my friend. The evidence is that on one of the trips to America, your wife went to the bank and withdrew an amount..."

"But the amount..."

"Don't say it was paltry. A half dollar...One dollar...a million dollars...The point is that you violated the law. We won't refer you to the prosecutors, since the case is trivial and your defense will persuade the prosecution. You will say that it is possible to consider the account closed since the amount left in it is paltry and you didn't deposit anything in it after you left. Therefore we will speak to Public Opinion. Mr. Public Opinion, this man who works as head of the Labor Party and as Prime Minister violated the law. Do with him as you will."

The phantom of Public Opinion arose with a rage and gave Rabin an intimidating eye from which sparks flew. Rabin conceded the leadership of the party to Peres, and in the next elections the Labor Party lost. In came the extremists led by Begin, costing Israel dearly, and us as well.

The Song and the Singer

The song is in Hebrew but the tune is familiar. Have I heard it before? Where?

I was riding in a taxi with Helal Gabriel, a journalist for an American newspaper. There is no need to meet in the hotel, I thought. "Helal, let's go to a place near the sea." On the road to the beach, the driver was playing this song on his car cassette player. A young man was singing, the melody was sad and beautiful, with a sweet, consoling refrain.

Should I ask the driver for the name of the song and singer? No need, for I have now retained the tune by singing it in my mind. I will go to a cassette shop and sing the refrain to the salesman. We got out of the taxi and walked a little while I hummed the refrain. We crossed the street, sat down in a cafe, and the tune disappeared from my mind. I should have asked the driver! Suddenly the tune returned again but in another form, wearing different garb. Yes...I know that tune, it's "I Missed You" by the Lebanese singer Ragheb Allamah. Yes, it certainly is the same tune, but in a new and beautiful delivery.

I'd known that there are Egyptian tunes sung in Hebrew, but it's one thing to hear of something and quite another to experience it. While I was talking with Helal my mind turned to the topic of the Israeli cultural invasion of Egypt. It is a hot issue among Egyptian intellectuals. But who is invading whom? And with what weapons? Where are the casualties, the prisoners, and then the cease-fire in this cultural invasion?

In the past, the cries of alarm against a cultural invasion were generally directed against the West. Now the cries of alarm more narrowly warn of an Israeli cultural invasion, which will happen while Arabs are "scurrying towards peace."[20]

The use of metaphors and symbols in speaking of reality conceals reality itself. We falsely depict life, and treat this fabricated depiction as if it were life itself. When the depiction is full of phantoms, then we waste our lives building fortresses and citadels to defend ourselves against them.

"Now that Israel has failed to invade us militarily, prepare to confront the cultural invasion."

"What is the plan of attack?"

"In all likelihood, Israel will launch Hebrew banners into the skies over

Arab capitals and scald us by pouring ashes from them. They will mount Hebrew novels on rockets so as to penetrate our minds and hearts and souls, and expel from them the works of not only Naguib Mahfouz, Taha Hussein and Ahmad Bahaeddin but also al-Mutanabbi and al-Jahiz and even the complaints of the Eloquent Peasant.[21] As for Hebrew melodies, Ariel Sharon himself will lead them in a swift pincer movement to encircle our hearts, destroying the melodies of al-Sunbati, al-Qassabgi, Abdel Wahhab and Baligh Hamdi.[22] Israel will launch its short history inside a nuclear eraser, capable of wiping out your own history full of creativity and wisdom."

"Oh, what a wretched, powerless victim am I! How can I protect myself from this invasion? What should I do to confront these lethal weapons?"

"Don't speak with them, listen to them or read them. Convince yourself that they don't exist. In your imagination, Israel is the temptress of the folk tales, the voice of seduction leading you to desire and destruction, the siren of Greek mythology and of the Thousand and One Nights. Hers is a captivating song, she possesses an enchanting voice which will lure you away and pull you to the bottom of the Nile. Plug your ears and become deaf. While you're at it, blind your eyes too, since a nuclear film or something like it could invade you..."

"Okay, I'll plug my ears and blind my eyes to protect me from the cultural invasion."

"But this is not enough my friend! They will attack with advanced new weapons capable of penetrating your mind without passing through your ears or eyes."

"Oh, what a lost orphan am I! What should I do to protect my mind?"

"Shut it, shut your mind. That's the solution."

"Okay, I've closed it."

"Now your ears are plugged, your eyes are closed and your mind is shut. But — praise the Lord — you are certainly saved from the Israeli cultural invasion. Now you are secure in your own heritage and your national and ethnic culture."

***

Several weeks before my travel to Israel, Dr. Galal Amin, a professor of political science at the American University in Cairo, came to the weekly evening gathering with Naguib Mahfouz. Amin is an intellectual with whom one is able to differ in a civilized way, without his thinking of slaughtering you or his beseeching God to strike you dead. He spoke at length about the dangers of the imminent Israeli cultural invasion that threatens Egypt's heritage and culture. Naguib Mahfouz listened to him and waited for him to finish, then asked: "Do you actually think Israel is capable of doing this to us?"

"Yes, that's why I came to ask you what we should do?"

"Die. If Israel is capable of annihilating the artistic, literary, and cultural heritage of Egypt and the Arab world, then we'd better all die."

Naguib Mahfouz seemed to realize that his reply was severe, so he continued in his well-known gentleness: "My dear, the issue in short is that now you are free to make your own decisions, after many long years in which there was someone else who bore the responsibility of making decisions. The intellectual in Egypt was working under the protection of an umbrella of prepared thought, which the regime built to protect us from the burning sun of freedom. This is what frightens you and all of us now. We are free to take our own decisions."

Afterwards I spoke with Dr. Galal of Peres's book *The New Middle East* and requested that he read it. He appeared exasperated or perhaps wary of the cultural invasion. However, as a university professor, he had an influential position requiring that he read a book of his enemy, so he assured me that he would read it. At the end of our conversation I could no longer refrain from exploding a bomb of a heavy type: "Read it for a very special reason. He quotes from the work of your brother Doctor Hussein."

He shouted in dismay: "My brother Doctor Hussein?"

"Yes, and among his other sources are the works of Doctor Irian and Doctor Sa'id al-Naggar and the poems of Nizar Qabbani."

***

People in Israel watch an Egyptian film subtitled in Hebrew on Israeli television at exactly five-thirty every Friday afternoon. They watch subtitled Egyptian serial dramas as well. To my knowledge, we haven't heard one Israeli warn of an Egyptian cultural invasion nor have we heard of victims of such an invasion.

The Israeli television official who broadcasts these films and TV dramas is not an Egyptian spy who has infiltrated across the border in order to impose our theater on them. He is an official who knows what his audience likes.

Dina, a Jew of Iraqi origin who works as photographer, told me: "I love Egyptian films. They have a very particular manner of treating the problems of human beings, they make me very happy. However, since I visited Egypt, I can say that you are much better than your films."

On my way home I stopped at a gas station in a desert area near the border with Egypt. There were two teenage boys with whom I failed to make my self understood either in Arabic or English. I said to them: "I am an Egyptian."

One of them shouted with joy: "Mitsrayim?"[23] His mind was searching quickly for a word or two of Arabic to build a bridge between us. Suddenly he shouted: "Makhmoud Yassin."

He pronounced the name with a Hebrew "kh" and communicated the message that he watches Egyptian films and knows their stars.

***

The talk of an Israeli cultural invasion of Egypt is nonsense, words that insult Egyptian culture and Egyptian intellectuals. It is an illusory phantom born of a feeling of inadequacy and an ignorance of the Egyptian and Israeli cultures. It is a stupid slogan chanted for demagogic purposes, remote from any consideration of Egyptian national interest. It creates an atmosphere of tumult and blackmail among intellectuals, and sows fear without justification among the young generation. They are still in search of the truth and of themselves, at the beginning of their literary and artistic paths. This atmosphere consigns them to misery and despair, affects their production, and strips them of the power and creativity which are the fruit of an accurate perception of reality.

Thus the slogan of cultural invasion becomes the white flag raised by those who have decided to surrender to the peace movement, owing to their inability to challenge it using their old rhetoric. Defeat becomes victory and victory defeat. Cowards are brave and weakness is strength.

***

Egyptians might have lost a lot, and might be deprived of many things, but one thing they will always have — "the cultural and spiritual leadership" of the region, according to Yitzhak Bar-Moshe in his book *Egypt in My Heart*. He gives a simple reason for this: "No one on earth can deprive Egypt of preserving its 'voice of place' or of re-exporting it."

Every place on earth has its voices, its special melodies and chants. Its physical features are also voices and echoes. From all of these together its culture and identity are formed. In Israel several races of human beings came from distant places and introduced their special melodies from the places where they were born and raised. Even historical facts and time periods have their voices. Many Israelis will not have heard the voice of Umm Kulthoum, they will not have enjoyed Egyptian drama or Egyptian actors. If you presented them a treasury of songs composed by al-Ghazali, Abdel Wahhab and Farid al-Atrash, they would politely decline to accept them. But here in Israel there are Muslim and Christian Arabs. And there are also Jewish Arabs. Yes, there are Jewish Arabs just as I am a Muslim Arab and Emile Habibi is a Christian Arab. They carry in their pockets Israeli identity cards and passports, and carry in their hearts Arab feelings which the voices of place have created.

Passports indicate an identity but do not create it. They are a contrivance to present to passport officials at airports or seaports. Identity cards are likewise needed to show to a bank official in order to cash a check, or to a policeman who suspects that you are someone else. Identity is something very different. It is thousands of layers created by the voices of place and time, compressed one on the other inside a human being. At a seminar in the Druze village of Hurfeish north of Haifa, Sami Michael said: "When I visit Cairo I kiss it as if I am kissing Baghdad." Samih al-Qasim said: "They play a lot on the tune that Druze are not Arabs...Who are we then? Frenchmen?"

Yaacov Setty, the press attache at the Israeli Embassy in Cairo, had told me: "If Saddam Hussein would allow Jews to visit Iraq, my father would walk to Baghdad on foot."

"But what about religion?" you ask.

Religion is a basic element of identity but not one's entire identity. We all belong to this place, and we keep deep inside us the voices of this part of the earth. As for me, I don't need to search in the dictionary for the meaning of the word 'Sephardim' to know that it includes Jewish Arabs, as well as Jewish Iranians and Bukharans. My references stand before me, vibrant with life. My references are people as I see them.

I began to notice this from the moment in the cafeteria when the Iraqi woman greeted me with such joy, then the Moroccan Jewish youth in the hotel restaurant who treated me in that affectionate way, then all the Jewish Arabs whom I met. Do you remember the story of the old-fashioned Upper Egyptian who was ready to lay down his life for a person connected to his home town? I am their home town.

"But the Oriental Jews whom you call Arabs, they treated our POWs the most cruelly at the front. And they usually vote for religious extremist parties, despite the fact that they are 'Arabs' as you call them."

Yes, but you are making a simple mistake. Don't say "in spite of the fact that they are Arabs" but rather "because they are Arabs." Indeed the best evidence that they are Arabs in their bones is exactly what you mentioned. Is there anyone more cruel to an Arab than another Arab? There is no need to be ashamed of this fact. What do you think of the way the Iraqi Arabs treated the Kuwaiti Arabs?

"War is war, war turns people into monsters."

I might agree with you, but what do you think of the way the other Arabs treat Egyptian workers in the Gulf, while as you know we are at peace with everyone?

"If the Oriental Jews are Arabs as you claim, then why do they vote for religious parties that are hostile to Arabs?"

For a simple, clear reason: they want to cause trouble for and fight against the Arab governments, which they hate just as we Arabs living in the Arab region do. In this matter they don't differ from you or me. Answer me honestly, assume an opportunity presented itself to cause trouble for the Arab governments publicly, wouldn't you take advantage of it?

Now, after we have learned of their identity, are we not enjoined to reconsider our way of dealing with the Arab-Israeli peace process? Indeed, spiritual, cultural and artistic supplies are already imported from Egyptian storerooms for the benefit of large sections of people there. We are exporting to them the voices of place, because we ourselves are the place itself. There is a role awaiting Egypt in Israel and Palestine now, and every moment that we delay affects not only the path of Palestinian-Israeli peace but also the steps towards Arab-Israeli peace.

No one mentions the word "Oslo" now in speaking about peace. The word has disappeared from circulation and become the property of historians. The name everyone mentions now in reference to Palestinian-Israeli agreements is the "Cairo Agreement."[24] The role of Cairo does not end, and must not be allowed to end, in closing the curtains on the stage of conference halls. Egypt's role begins after the curtains are closed, it begins on the ground in the West Bank and Israel. I say on the ground and not in the halls of the foreign ministries of the two countries or in dimly lit rooms, but rather in the full light of day, in the streets, city squares, neighborhoods, universities, among intellectuals and on television and radio programs. We should say: We came from Cairo to protect the Cairo Agreement. We must support the current Palestinian leadership, despite what we may think of its shortcomings, so that its rivals know that it doesn't stand alone. We must also support the Labor Party because if the Likud comes to power in Israel in the next elections, then we can say to the entire region "May you rest in peace."

"These are dangerous words...You ask not only for normal relations between Egypt and Israel, you want us to support the Israeli government."

Yes, support the Labor Party. In any case, I thank you for not shouting in my face: "How much did you take from Rabin?"

"The Big Night" in Jerusalem and Sorrow in Jericho

"Believe me my dear Gaby, I will be with you, God willing, at the Arabic literature department of the Hebrew University in Jerusalem at exactly twelve o'clock noon next Monday."

"Where will you stay in Jerusalem?"

"I don't know at the moment. I asked a friend to reserve a hotel room there, and he hasn't called me yet."

"How will you get to the university? It resembles a maze and is spread out over several locations. We are at Mount Scopus."

"Gaby, write me the address in Hebrew, Arabic and English."

He did so and departed, not believing that I would fulfill my promise to him.

***

"Hello Ali. It's Abdallah Ovadiah. I reserved a room for you in Jerusalem at the Moriah Hotel."

"Thank you Abdallah. Is it a three-star?"

"No, it has many stars...more than you imagine, and an underground garage so you can feel at ease about your car. Don't concern yourself with the stars, you are my guest. But I advise you to make long-distance telephone calls outside the hotel, and also not to order anything from room service. The prices in the hotel are very high."

Abdallah clearly believes that the financial situation of Egyptian playwrights is extremely bad. In addition, he himself hates mediocre hotels. When he goes to Cairo with Sami Michael and Sasson Somekh, he leaves them in a four-star hotel and resides in a five-star.

I myself feel strange in this sort of hotel, as if I am living in an amusement park. The employees in these hotels treat you with a false sort of *politesse*, as if to make you feel at every moment that they are from a higher social class than you, or that they are making a great concession to permit you to stay at their establishment. For them you are merely a key bearing a room number, while in small hotels you are closer to being a guest. I didn't listen to Abdallah's warning about not using the hotel's facilities. Since I did not pay the price for a night's sleep, I was willing to pay the price of wakefulness. I am generous with myself and with my guests.

***

"Hello...My name is Dana, one of Professor Sasson's students. I attended your lecture at the university. My friend Shira and I would like to meet you."

Dana and Shira were slightly over twenty years of age. Dana resembles to an astonishing extent my younger daughter. She has a childish face, rejoicing in childhood and at the same time enjoying a large amount of responsibility. She works as a reviewer at a publishing house, rewriting language. Most likely she acquired her elevated verbal sense from her mother, who works as a translator from English into Hebrew. As for Shira, her dark complexion bespeaks her Moroccan roots. She has Asian features surmounted with a permanent smile which mixes gentleness and good nature. She is mature to the extent of being able to make fun of herself in a natural way. She spoke of her mother's culinary talents with Moroccan dishes. She was silent a moment and then added: "I am sure that the boys who went out with me were attracted not to my black eyes, but rather to my mother's cooking."

They came with me from Tel Aviv to Jerusalem. I needed someone to show me the way in Jerusalem to the hotel so that I could find it directly, after the enjoyable feeling of lingering in a new city had passed. I was concerned about my family. I failed to reach them by telephone, and learned later that they took it off the hook to avoid being pestered by journalists.

In Jerusalem they called a girlfriend, Sagit, who also studied Arabic, and she came with her boyfriend, Ofer, about thirty years of age, a doctoral candidate in physics. I didn't feel strange at all with this group, as if I had known them for years. We went to the promenade overlooking Jerusalem from a towering height, and the city was transformed into hills of green gardens interspersed with buildings. We went to the Old City, passing through the great stone walls of the Damascus Gate. For a moment I found myself in Khan al-Khalili in Cairo or the Arab Market in Tunis. At a certain point in the narrow crowded roads, Sagit said: "Let's go back now. It's dangerous to go further in this direction. Some Jews were stabbed with knives in this area."

Ofer replied calmly: "Continue walking, Sagit."

Ofer is a member of an Arab-Jewish group that works for peace. His roommate is an Arab youth named Saber. Ofer's family has lived in Haifa for hundreds of years. I believe his calm and composure result from deep feelings that he has roots in this land just like the Arabs. He doesn't fear them. This is his land, his and his Muslim and Christian colleagues. Even if a detestable incident occurs, he is obliged to accept it as he would accept fate. He is obliged to pay the price for defending peace even if there is a knife stabbing.

Ofer doesn't speak much. We didn't speak about the Arab-Israeli conflict or about peace. Sometimes you meet someone who believes in all that you believe, and you walk together free to enjoy each other's company and comradeship. You are members of the same club, the club of life.

The only question he asked with interest and enthusiasm was: "Ali, do you play backgammon?"

"Yes."

"Prisoner Backgammon?"

"It's difficult, Ofer, to find an Egyptian who doesn't know all the varieties of backgammon."

My answer satisfied him. In the evening, I was surprised that he came to the hotel carrying a backgammon board under his arm. Clearly the poor man had been searching for several years for a backgammon partner.

Is Ofer a brave man?

And what is bravery?

I don't think bravery is challenging danger, or the absence of fear, or the ability to brush it aside. Rather, it is the capacity to handle danger gently, to feel fear without letting it spoil your life or turn you into someone you don't want to be.

We were now in the heart of the Arab section of Jerusalem, an Arab and four Jews. We took lunch at a *kabab* grill. "Chef, do you have liver?"

"No, sorry."

I went out and bought a big piece of liver from a nearby butcher. I asked the *kabab* chef to grill it and he welcomed the idea. I knew that this was an unusual request outside of the traditions of *kabab* joints, but I was certain that he would welcome the idea since I was an Egyptian guest and not a regular customer.

I insisted on paying the bill, but Ofer placed some bills in my pocket calmly and firmly without opening his mouth. A large quantity of liver and *kabab* remained on the table so I said: "Can you imagine us leaving all this food?"

We asked for some loaves of bread and the girls were occupied with making sandwiches and putting them in a big plastic sack. Ofer insisted on giving me the sack.

"Ofer, I don't have a refrigerator in the hotel. You keep it and I'll come visit you."

That night he and Sagit came with the sack of sandwiches and the backgammon board. He said that Dana and Shira had returned to Tel Aviv...he brought the sandwiches so we could have dinner together.

It was the only evening on the trip that I spent in a hotel. Sagit sat silently watching television while Ofer and I played backgammon. Ofer the Silent was astonished at the verbal campaign which I launched at him during the game. Backgammon is nearly the only game Egyptians cannot play silently. An aggressive verbal campaign must accompany each toss of the dice or movement of the pieces, even in the case of defeat. "I gave you that round in my giving mood in order to encourage you to keep playing. Now, you hero, prepare for the blitzkrieg."

Or in a similar vein: "Have you had enough training? Did you study backgammon in a special institute? Are you a professional? Please watch your fingers, because I now will play in a style known as Earthquake 15." Et cetera.

***

When going to a place I have never been before, I generally arrive long before the time of the appointment. But Gaby was right that the Hebrew University building on Mount Scopus resembled a maze. The architect was seized with the idea of a fortress, with circular passageways and stairways branching off from each other in different directions. Arriving at the intended place resembled the difficult tasks assigned to the heroes of ancient tales. The signs, arrows and color-coded hallways merely made the matter more difficult.

Finally I met Gaby near the department. He hadn't informed his students that I was coming. He said he wanted to surprise them with my presence. I believe he was not certain that I would fulfill my promise, or perhaps his prior experience suggested that no one on the face of the earth could arrive at the Arabic language department of their own power. The lecture hall was packed. When Gaby and I entered one of the Arab students shouted: "Ali Salem...I saw you on television...Do you remember me? I sat with you at Cafe Riche some years ago."

Gaby began to lecture with a wide smile. He spoke of the different ways of pronouncing the Arabic letter *qaf* when it comes at the end of a word, in the dialects of Cairo and of Upper Egypt. Gaby chose to illustrate his point with the poetry of "The Big Night" written by the late Salah Jahin, and set to music by Sayyid Makawy, may God grant him long life. He distributed a paper with several verses of "The Big Night" and turned on a large cassette player.

The Aragoz:[25] "Keep going straight ahead, straight ahead until you come across a building."

"Listen well to the Aragoz pronouncing the dialect of people from Cairo and you will notice him saying *ma tela'i emarah* (until you come across a building). Now listen to the response of the village chief from Upper Egypt, *ma alagi emareh* (until I come across a building). The *qaf* here is pronounced with a 'g' and the final 'a' of *emarah* becomes 'e'." The students listened while Gaby continued his explanation.

Gaby said to me: "Last year I taught all of 'The Big Night' and my students sang it in the university courtyard and cafeteria, among hundreds of students startled by the beauty of its melodies."

Mrs. Ella Aphek of the Israeli Foreign Ministry attended the lecture and took photographs of me with the students in the lecture hall. We moved to a different hall where the lecture was on the Egyptian theater. Gaby spoke a long time about the theater, and then asked me to read to them a long scene from the play of Tawfiq al-Hakim, "A Bullet in the Heart," and then several scenes from my play "You are the One Who Killed the Monster."

The subject of Gaby's doctoral dissertation, which he has not yet submitted, is dialogue in the Egyptian theater. His selection of scenes for me to read indicated his deep understanding of his subject. When you read the Egyptian colloquial of Tawfiq al-Hakim in "A Bullet in the Heart," then read or listen to the colloquial written by the serious dramatists now, you suddenly discover that it has acquired a high level of purity, music, concentration and eloquence. The colloquial language has risen to a level that permits it to present a wonderful musical depiction like "The Big

Night." The long-standing battle between colloquial and classical Arabic is false and illusory. What's important is to achieve a pure language capable of reaching quickly and gently to the heart.

"I came on a trip of peace, in support of Arab-Israeli peace and the Agreement for Gaza-Jericho First."

An Arab student in the front row whispered: "First and last."

His comment provoked me. "My dear, I don't want to talk about politics. Why do you pull me into it? But no matter. You don't agree then with this peace."

"That's right."

"Why not?"

"I don't see it as just."

"What are you doing to make it just? What is the role you will play to obtain a just peace? After Camp David, some Egyptian intellectuals said: 'Israel won't carry out its commitments to withdraw from Sinai.' After it withdrew to the first line, from al-Arish to Ras Muhammad, they said Israel would not complete the withdrawal, that this was all we would obtain. Then it withdrew according to the agreement to the international borders. Now you say Gaza-Jericho first and last, meaning that this is all the Palestinians will obtain. Let's assume now that your prediction is correct. What will you do to avoid this? What will you do so that this will be the first and not the last?

"We should not take lightly the words which glorify despair and grant us the opportunity to enjoy inaction and intellectual laziness. Put yourself in the place of the Palestinian and Israeli negotiators. Each side is full of apprehension, doubt and caution, fearing to move one millimeter without considering all the political trends among their people. You should come forward and help them to build the necessary trust to create peace. Come forward to create peace, not to speak of or comment on it negatively. Come forward to remove the fear, doubt and caution. Any questions?"

An Arab woman sitting in the back row said: "There's no democracy in Egypt."

"Miss, I am not here to defend the system or the government in Egypt. But I say to you, despite the explicit and implicit aggression towards Israel among Egyptian intellectuals and the media, which does threaten the supporters of peace by silencing them, I say to you despite all this that we have enough democracy to allow me to come here and to return home without suffering from any mishaps. The extent of democracy in Egypt allows me this."

"President Mubarak attained a third term."

"Yes, at the ballot box and not with tanks. The Egyptians chose him. Once more, I am not here to defend President Mubarak or the Egyptian government. I say to you clearly: to the extent there is democracy in the Arab region, then we in Egypt enjoy a higher degree of it than anywhere else. Please don't understand that we are content with this. There are many liberals in Egypt fighting every moment to obtain more freedom. I assure you that we are gaining increments of freedom and democracy all the time. We will continue on this path until we achieve the democracy we dream of, because we know the only way to raise our standard of living is first to establish peace.

"Any other questions? Thank you, may peace be with you and with us, and God's peace, compassion and blessings upon us all."

***

Ofer and his girlfriend Sagit invited me to a party at the home of a Jewish lawyer dedicated to defending Arabs. The occasion for the party was the achievement of democracy in South Africa.

In a working-class neighborhood of Moroccan Jews, we entered the lawyer's two-storey home. It was filled top to bottom with Jewish and Arab youth of both sexes. At every festive occasion in the world, a large number of human beings immerse themselves in enjoying the moment while a small group isolated in a corner struggles against the festive mood. I sat with the latter group on the balcony of the house. Imagining that I was in Israel by official invitation, they began attacking everything governmental and official. A young woman said to me: "I directed a film about Umm Kulthoum and a film about Muhammad Abdel Wahhab,[26] and sold a copy to French television and another to Israeli television."

"That's nice."

We were speaking in English and she replied angrily: "No it's not. They broadcast the films only on the Arabic channel in Israel."

"Madame, that's only natural, the audience for these films, Israeli Arabs, watch that channel."

She once again said sharply: "The Arabs and the Sephardic Jews already know Umm Kulthoum and Abdel Wahhab well. They should have broadcast them on the main Hebrew language channel. I want to present this type of culture to the Jews of European origin."

The danger of this kind of argument is to find oneself gradually entering a debate of no interest and in which one has no position. I said to her delicately: "If you were the director of programming of the television station, would you agree to broadcast a kind of art that is very distant from the taste of your viewers? Or would you put it on a channel whose audience enjoys this type of art? But what do I know about Israeli television? Tell me which songs of Umm Kulthoum you like?"

I tried to turn the sharp argument to song but failed. An Arab youth caught the rope and asked sullenly: "Where is the peace which you came to support?"

Then Ofer became irritated and shouted: "You apparently think that the man was invited by the Israeli government, or was sent by the Egyptian government and that I am his official escort."

I interrupted the discussion: "Ofer, please. The man asked a question and I am obliged to answer. You wondered about the character of the peace I came to support? It is the peace which lives now in this moment. Moments ago you were all Jews and Arabs celebrating an historical occasion, surrounded by food, drink and joy in the home of a Jewish woman entrusted with filing cases for Palestinians who are imprisoned or persecuted. Aren't these moments of peace that include all of you here? Do you think it impossible that others can achieve these moments?"

"I don't say it's impossible to achieve peace...But I oppose the way which it is being done. It isn't just. There must be another way."

"Would you like to explain it to us? You have nothing except opposition. Your words, sir, are not new to me. I have heard them hundreds of times. Your lexicon is the same as that used throughout the entire Arab region. Your behavior is also the same, denying the fruits of peace and working to deprive others of them. Or at least strongly opposing when others get close to these fruits."

Ofer said to him: "I listened carefully to you. You don't see any hope, everything around you is bad. The efforts of Israeli and Palestinian people won't achieve peace. What is the solution then? What should we do?"

Before matters reached a crisis, the hostess entered and moderated the atmosphere. We said good-bye and departed. A Jewish youth named

Sami, one of Ofer's friends, accompanied us to the car. While shaking my hand good-bye he said: "Ali, don't think badly of these guys and don't denigrate them. I agree with you that their views are extreme. But over many years they have worked seriously to force the Israeli government to recognize the rights of the Palestinian people."

"Believe me, I don't denigrate them. But I was waiting for an awareness from them that there are historical moments that put an end to extremist views. And there are other moments that require us to clasp to the rays of hope and strive to turn them into a burning flame, lighting life for all. Ideas that don't translate into actions that build trust between people and build life lack any importance. What really irritated me was to see a group of Arab and Jewish intellectuals celebrating in Jerusalem the victory of freedom in Johannesburg, then hear one of the group speak to me of the impossibility of peace."

On our way back to the hotel Ofer said to me: "I also have crazy Jewish friends. Imagine that they ask me with disgust: 'How can you be secure sleeping under the same roof as an Arab?' I tell them that he is my friend for the past twelve years. They say: 'Aren't you afraid he will stab you while you are sleeping?'"

"The battle is long, Ofer. It's easier to dear a minefield than to clear a human heart of hatred and terror."

***

It was early afternoon. "Ofer, will you come with me to Jericho?"

He replied without hesitation: "Yes, when?"

"Now."

The distance between Jerusalem and Jericho was twenty-five kilometers. The road was desolate and dangerous, winding between desert hills. Before entering it we stopped at a military checkpoint. I showed them my passport and Ofer showed his ID card.

Listen carefully about Jericho before going to see it. It is a very small city. I felt constrained and sensed despair and misery as we entered it. There were several small shops, a restaurant and cafe at the entrance to the city, and a small number of people who have not smiled for generations. The slogans written hastily in black paint on all the walls announced in an ugly way the reality of dissension among the Palestinian organizations.

It resembled a small city exposed to a violent air attack that had irradiated it with poverty. The few groups of people on the street were surprised to see an Egyptian car, and they waved in welcome. All the shops on the main street were closed except one, and its owner invited us for coffee. With him was a young man who welcomed us and began to speak.

"There is nothing here...Nothing to buy or sell. No work. We are passing through black times."

"Are these shops closed all the time?"

"No, people are accustomed to take a mid-afternoon nap. Sleep is the one activity allowed to us now. I graduated with a bachelor's degree in commerce. Now I sell fruit. Every morning I bring several kilograms of fruit and sell it."

We were sitting on the sidewalk in front of the shop — the shop owner, the young man, Ofer and I. A military jeep with three soldiers passed in front of us every few minutes. It was a very small city. A tour of the city's landmarks, which lasted several minutes, confirmed this conclusion. We went to a tourist site, a few excavated archeological mounds. It appeared to have occupied a place in history whose importance I have forgotten. There were some German tourists there and dozens of young boys trying to sell them touristic souvenirs. All of history and all of its sites and places can go to hell. There is nothing on earth more important than man.

I was filled with despair, and began to recall a sentence of President Sadat's. "We want to begin raising the suffering of the Palestinian people." Yes, this is suffering. The people here are not imprisoned or in detention but they are suffering from something worse, the inability to live in the heart of life itself.

"This is the villa of President Arafat. They say the reception hall cost one hundred thousand dollars."

The rumors have begun.

"Our situation was different when we were allowed to work in Israel. We earned a lot of money."

Yes, my dear. But nothing of what you earned is reflected in Jericho. Cities are containers for human beings, they are also our partners in gain and loss, wealth and poverty, happiness and misery. Here I see a partner only in poverty and despair.

My anger over this misery certainly made me blame its inhabitants. During an occupation people think only of staying alive. When they are unable to pay the price of staying alive, they immediately think of ending it. There are numerous ways of doing this; one is death, their death and the death of others.

The atmosphere of poverty and torpor made me fearful and the sight of human misery made me lose my sense of security. Initially I had wanted to stay until evening, to sit and talk with the local personages at the cafe. But I feared driving at night to Jerusalem, the road didn't inspire confidence. So we left Jericho before sundown. On the way back I didn't exchange a word with Ofer. I was miserable, as if a large part of the sadness of the city had infiltrated my mind and settled in my heart.

The road was in fact dangerous. It was on this same road that the poet Tawfiq Ziyad died in a car accident several months later.

Oh, my beloved Tawfiq, how quickly grew a love which now has turned to grief.

In The Matter of Meat and Bones

A meeting in Mishkenot Shaananim, an old building in Jerusalem surrounded by gardens, where they receive creative people from all over the
world. It is also used as a guest residence. The meeting included a number
of literary figures, among them the great poet Yehuda Amichai, in addition to Dr. Matityahu Peled, who is a lecturer in Arabic literature at Tel
Aviv University and a former general, Professor Sasson Somekh, and two
former Israeli ambassadors to Egypt, Moshe Sasson and Shimon Shamir.
The latter had resigned his post in protest of the policies of Prime Minister Yitzhak Shamir, and returned to work as a university professor.

Professor Somekh asked me to speak in Arabic since most of the
attendees understood it well. Among the things I said was that I couldn't
imagine myself visiting Israel during the Shamir government, just as I
could not imagine Israel without the Labor Party.

The newspaper *Davar*[27] published this sentence in a long article and
the editor added: "We cite this without comment." I hope that I didn't
overstep the bounds of decorum. I take comfort in the fact that I think it
is true, and believe that the Likud didn't create peace between Egypt and
Israel. Rather, peace was achieved despite the presence of the Likud,
thanks to Sadat's powers of endurance and Carter's honesty.

The Likud Party and its short-sighted geniuses are responsible for all
the disasters which are now occurring to the Palestinians and Israelis. I
hope no one considers this interference in the domestic affairs of the Israeli voter. I am giving my opinion as one of the residents of the region.
The Likud has planted mines without a map in the field of peace, and it
won't be possible to remove them without thousands of additional Palestinian and Israeli victims.

***

Moshe Sasson said: "Some of your intellectuals speak of the 'scurrying'
of Arab countries towards peace. Fifteen years after signing the peace
agreement and they speak of 'scurrying?'"

Dr. Matityahu Peled gave me his study in English of the Arab writer
Ahmad Faris al-Shidiyaq, then asked me one question: "Will the Muslim
fundamentalists achieve power in Egypt?"

"No."

"Why not?"

"The Egyptian military establishment won't allow them to do this."

"Even if..."

"Even if everything, sir."

What I didn't tell Professor Peled is that the psychological and cultural orientation of the Egyptian military over the course of history is to protect Egypt's borders. The military works on the ground and doesn't float among the clouds of foggy thoughts. Egyptian military men certainly learned more than anyone else from Iran's experience. The legitimate power of the state in Iran made its last appearance in the office of Prime Minister Bakhtiar, when he held a meeting for the generals of the Iranian army on the day following Imam Khomeini's arrival. Not one of them came to the meeting. The man waited two hours until the news arrived that at that very moment the generals were sitting in the front row of the mosque listening to the Imam's sermon. The compass of stupid opportunism led them to the wrong places, and in the next scene all of their bodies lay in a large morgue refrigerator.

Safeguarding the borders is the chief obsession of the Egyptian military establishment. Oddly enough, among the decisive pieces of evidence in the Taba arbitration between Israel and Egypt[28], according to my understanding, were several old photographs kept by a retired army officer. He took pictures of his soldiers when he was a young man serving at this spot on the border with Israel. He undoubtedly lost many pictures from his album, but did he lose these pictures with the features of Egypt's borders in the background?

The psychological motivation that drove the officer to keep those pictures goes beyond the traditional preservation of memories. The same kind of motivation leads to defending the borders.

I can only understand Sadat's initiative in going to Jerusalem, with all of its strangeness, in light of this psychological composition of the Egyptian officer. He is prepared to do anything for the sake of reclaiming his land and returning to his borders. Of course Sadat was aware of the savage, terrifying campaign which awaited him both inside Egypt and throughout the Arab world. But none of this dissuaded him from his purpose. Returning to the borders was his personal honor and his psychological satisfaction. As for all these expressions against him, they had no importance.

When you do something that leads you to your psychological makeup, you do it with contentment, certainty and creativity. This explains Sadat's singular certainty when he addressed the Knesset. Without understanding the psychological aspects of the Egyptian military establishment, it is impossible to understand what Sadat did. In his memoirs of the Camp David talks, Muhammad Ibrahim Kamel, Egypt's foreign minister at the time, made fun of Sadat for telling him: "Allow me, Muhammad, to eat the meat and afterwards I will suck on the bones at my leisure." Kamel made a terrible mistake in not understanding the political meaning of this strange sentence, which only the Egyptian peasant would understand.

Sadat was in the final analysis a peasant invited to a village banquet. A number of people are seated around a low round table and in front of them is an enormous platter filled with country stew. On top of the stew is large mass of meat mixed with bones. All of them pretend to be preoccupied in conversation and chit chat, and not interested in fighting over the meat. But the peasant who knows the rules well can slowly gobble up the meat before the others eat any. Afterwards he can join in the chatting and storytelling while sucking on the bones.

Indeed, the return of Sinai was the meat. But he didn't depart from his seat. He continued to negotiate for the sake of the Palestinian people, after acquiring credibility and an elevated position in the eyes of the world as a maker of peace, which assured him of success in these negotiations. Thus we find Ezer Weizman saying in his book on the peace agreement: "Sadat with his stammering English gained everything, while Begin in his eloquence lost us all of the issues." The Israeli writer Amos Elon described in his book a conversation between an Israeli journalist and a senior official. The journalist asks him in exasperation: "What will we learn from the Egyptians?"

The senior official answered: "Diplomacy."

"So," you say, "we have a separate peace with Israel then."

Ignorance of history together with hypocrisy are the reasons for feeling shame in announcing that our agreement with Israel is a separate peace. It would have been impossible practically, realistically, and legally to reach any other kind of agreement that would have included the return of our land and the achievement of peace. Didn't Nasser himself ask Jordan's King Hussein to work for the return of the West Bank in any manner he could?

Oh people, will we continue forever devising laws for a reality that doesn't in fact exist? What is this talk of collective action which has taken root in the minds of some of us?

The machinery of collectivity has crushed us and made us into one bloc. The features of individuality have completely disappeared. For many long years we have stood "all together" in front of the collective store waiting for any commodity; we gathered "all together" in the city squares to listen to the speeches of the leader; we held our breath "all together" waiting to hear important news that will be broadcast in a few minutes and will affect us "all together." We submitted our papers "all together" to the office of coordination, and waited "all together" to be spread out among the universities. Then we waited "all together" for an appointment, and waited "all together" for the Labor Day bonus and the holiday bonus. Finally we waited "all together" for the new retirement law.

As for Egyptian intellectuals from all the different political and ideological trends, they were arrested "all together" and tortured "all together" and set free "all together," then appointed "all together" to governmental positions.

My late friend Amal Dunkul said to me: "Every Egyptian youth has either been imprisoned or almost imprisoned." Those who managed to slip away did so by chance or by good fortune, and the writer of these lines is among them. Nevertheless, the opportunity is still available for those whose turn has not yet come up. There is no despair in life.

Things happened to us "all together" and why should peace with Israel be any different? Why shouldn't peace with Israel happen "all together" in one blow or in one agreement?

Any human being thinking normally or semi-normally knows for a certainty that a collective peace on this issue is impossible. Any one of the parties can, at the right time, cause the whole matter to fail, for peculiar regional or leadership calculations or because of a lack of responsibility.

What can we do with a leader who kidnapped a people and left them in a remote corner of history and began to eat their meat and suck on their bones at his leisure? What to do with a leader who succeeded with his astonishing wealth to provide his people with terror, misery and destruction?

What to do with heads of states and kingdoms whose thoughts, desires and interests I challenge you to truly know?

Finally, what to do with a head of state who actually wants peace but whose administrative machinery has for long years needed retooling, since it was constructed from the iron of war, barbed wire and hatred?

Do you expect them to sit down at the negotiating table and agree on any one thing? Should we have left Sinai for Israel? Left the millions of residents of the Suez Canal cities displaced from their homes? Should we have dispensed with the income from the Suez Canal? Should we have waited for a collective agreement that all of us are certain would be impossible?

"But Sadat took back the Sinai without gaining full sovereignty over it."

What do you mean, do you see yourself lacking sovereignty over Sinai?

"Of course. The Peace Agreement restricts the movement of our forces in Sinai."

Do you want to move your forces near the border of a state with which you signed a peace agreement?

"Of course."

Why? Do you intend to fight with the neighbor?

"No, but I want to exercise my sovereignty over all of Sinai."

The mistake then is not with the agreement but with your understanding of the word 'sovereignty.' The study of history tells us that armies should move only in two situations — maneuvers and wars. Moving an army to impart a feeling of sovereignty to oneself or to another is highly dangerous. This was our biggest mistake in 1967. We moved the tanks not for the sake of maneuvers or for war, and the rest is history.

Sovereignty is represented not by tanks but by laws and the ability to impose them on everyone. You are sovereign in the land when you bear the axe to protect the law inside your borders.[29] As for the rifle, you should only raise it when someone threatens to prevent you from bearing the axe and protecting the law. You will achieve full sovereignty over Sinai with the axe alone. It has taken many years to convince you to develop Sinai and settle it with civilians. There were clever articles claiming: "It is impossible strategically to defend Sinai. Should we build it up only to have Israel occupy it in the end?"

Oh, you far-sighted ones, the answer is yes, build up and make Sinai civilian precisely to exercise your sovereignty and deny it to others. Finally, the construction of Sinai has begun, in both its north and south and at an ever-increasing pace. The stupid opposition, with all its refinement and wittiness, has fallen silent.

Sadat did not take back Sinai without full sovereignty. Please, exercise sovereignty over it, but I remind you that this is very difficult because it requires you first to govern it. When you do this, you will be the sovereign of it and of every inch of the land of Egypt.

I Fight, Therefore I Am Killed

The shopping center in Jerusalem is said to be one of the largest in the world. In one of its many cafeterias a Palestinian youth stabbed two Israeli soldiers and fled with a companion, though local people managed to catch them. This incident and the others like it destroy the traditional Israeli concept of security.

A large number of older Israeli politicians thought that force was the only guarantee of security. They confused the concept of securing land from a military perspective with the concept of securing life for their citizenry. With force you can occupy a piece of land, but you will not be able to use force to occupy any part of the heart of your enemy. All the tanks in the world will fail to protect you from one person armed with hatred and loss and a desire to die. He will be able to reach you either with ease or difficulty.

Security is founded on legitimate right which power protects. Power by itself, as John Stuart Mill says, doesn't produce legitimate right. Some politicians in the modern era believe that the ancient philosophers have lost their value and validity and should no longer be considered great, like ancient oil lamps. Among them was Aristotle who wrote in *Politics* about the individual and the State. He said: "The State precedes the individual and human beings need the State." The only people capable of doing without the State must be either monsters or gods.

By turning this thought on its head and drawing on the data of reality, which is truer than any theory, we might say: As the State weakens, some people become monsters and others become gods, or they acquire both traits together.

But what happens when the State itself disappears? Isn't it inevitable that all people living in this situation become either monsters or gods? Isn't it possible to understand what has happened in the West Bank and Gaza and elsewhere in the Arab region in light of this idea?

Humankind needs the State to remain human, by which I mean the State characterized by justice, or what we call in the modern era political and economic freedom. Machiavelli discussed his concept of the castle and its connection with protecting the State. He concluded that the castle by itself doesn't protect the State. To protect the State the Prince must build a castle in the hearts of his people.

There is a brilliant saying in Menachem Begin's book *The Irgun*: "I fight, therefore I exist." This idea arises directly from the instinct of aggression, masquerading in the clothing of fighters defending their existence. Reality harshly refutes this idea and transforms it over time to: "I fight, therefore I exist — until you come along and end my existence with the stab of a knife or a charge of dynamite." The idea which extends throughout time is: "I fight in order to defend myself until we agree on peace...I want peace, therefore I exist, and you also exist when you want peace."

***

These thoughts turned in my mind as I sat in a cafeteria in Jerusalem's shopping center with Victor Nachmias, an Egyptian Jew from the Zahir neighborhood of Cairo. He had been a third-year student of pharmacology when he left Egypt. He didn't continue studying pharmacology, he studied media and now teaches "The Egyptian Media" at Tel Aviv University, in addition to working for an institution that collects donations from Jews throughout the world. He collects in one year about five hundred million dollars. To help you better understand their methodologies for collecting money, allow me to explain the project called "the blue box." Especially for Jewish children throughout the world, it involves placing small change in the box and sending it to Israel at the end of the year. They collect through this project alone thirty million dollars per year.

With Victor Nachmias and Meir Cohen, a television correspondent for the Arab region, I didn't feel that I was sitting with Egyptian Jews or Jewish Egyptians. I only felt I was sitting with Egyptian friends.

After the peace treaty between Egypt and Israel, Victor came to Egypt. At the time he was working for Israeli television and he came to make a television program about peace. He went to the Zahir neighborhood and asked the photographer to film what happened, without prior planning. He approached his house, the doorman was an old man sitting next to the house deep in sleep. Victor gently tapped his shoulder, the man opened his eyes, stared and shouted: "Biki!" Biki was the name that his family and neighborhood friends called him when he was a young man.

***

I asked an Egyptian working in television in Jerusalem: "Have you visited Egypt after the peace treaty?"

"Oh, I visited twelve times." How many times does the average expatriate Egyptian visit Egypt in the same period of time?

In a meeting with thirty-five persons at the Israeli Foreign Ministry, one asked me: "Egyptian Jews went out from Egypt twice, once in ancient times and the second in modern times. They had cultural activities in Egypt...Do you now miss this cultural activity?"

The questioner was sitting at the far end of the hall, and the lady sitting next to me whispered to me: "He is an Egyptian born in Egypt." I replied to her: "Madame, I know he is an Egyptian...I sense an Egyptian from afar."

I answered him: "I know that in fact they supported some cultural magazines. However, in answer to your question, I would reply that we do not now feel the loss of this activity. But I would say to you: The generations older than us, who were on intimate terms with Jews in Egypt, when they speak of the Jews they say: 'They were honest.'"

The strongest bridges of peace between Egypt and Israel are the Egyptian Jews. I don't precisely know how to benefit from their presence there, but I imagine that a conference for them in Cairo or Alexandria with the theme: "What do you want from Egypt?" would contribute decisively to building trust between the two peoples.

***

I left Jerusalem and went to Haifa and stayed two nights. I came to meet Sami Michael, and attended a birthday party for one of Sami's relatives in his sixties. The family welcomed me. The Jewish wife in her fifties is not the Jewish woman in her twenties. One can read on the faces of the older generation of Jewish women all the features of ancient hardship. But the younger generation is completely different. They work in all fields, including the military and the police. Some wear high boots with naked thighs, with the shortest possible skirts. The bodies are strong and healthy. It is strange that this nakedness doesn't summon in your mind the idea of the bed. To the contrary, it pushes you to think that there shouldn't occur any problem for this woman. All that you can think of is to distance yourself from her. She is a strong and beautiful human machine, her appearance inspiring the thought that she is capable of aggression.

There are of course Jewish women who wear traditional clothing, but in every case the Israeli woman is a first-class citizen. The entire society is aware that at the center of modesty is the intellect, and that moral dissolution also begins with the intellect before it announces itself in action. The thousand tons of paper that we scribble on to defend the rights of the Egyptian woman have no importance next to a decree that would state that Egyptian women may work in all fields, first and foremost the police and the military. Egyptian women used to serve in the police before a decree abolished this system. I say here clearly: That decree is irresponsible and unconstitutional.

***

We left the birthday party, Sami and I. A car was waiting to take us to the village of Hurfeish on the northern outskirts of Haifa. There was some road construction.

"Israel is preparing for peace with Syria...this road goes up to Damascus."

"Then may I live long, Sami, and travel from Cairo to Damascus on this road."

The seminar was held in a large high school auditorium. Attending it were Samih al-Qasim; Nazih Kheyr, a well-known critic and translator; Ada Aharoni, an Egyptian Jewish writer and university professor. The writer Nimr Nimr, who is from the village, led the discussion on culture and peace. Sami introduced me to the audience and I gave a short statement: "Many years ago my brother came to your borders riding a tank or an armored car and he did not return home.[30] Perhaps brothers or sons of yours went to the Egyptian borders riding tanks and did not return home. But I come to you in my car in order to show to Egyptians and Israelis that there is a common border between us. You are close to us and we to you. This region is no longer suitable for transportation by tank. The only way to ensure that our children return safely is to move in this part of the world by car and tractor. The trip is also a message to the generals of war that the time has come to pave the way for us, the generals of the written word, to make peace."

We returned to Haifa after midnight. Lights sparkling from high up in the villages adorned the mountains and hills with their intensity. The amount of light made me imagine that the mountains were celebrating in silence a big wedding, perhaps celebrating the marriage of some of the hills to each other.

The Sun on My Right

I left Haifa in the afternoon on my way south to the Egyptian border. I hate driving in cities, but I love long drives through the country since the features around me change at every moment as if I am making the changes. It allows my thoughts to flow freely. I have no illusions as to what awaits me in Cairo, I know what I'll confront. There is no end to the pain felt by most people when you suddenly raise their curtain of illusions and lies.

After the storm subsides, however, younger generations may consider my trip calmly and discover what I want them to discover — that the condition of mental war is defective and it obscures from us the sun of freedom and development. Between Israel and us there are no minefields, only the paved roads that I traveled.

My trip was extremely short, it didn't allow me to describe the Israelis any better than could a passenger traveling in a fast car past groups of people. Two nights in Netanya, one in Umm al-Fahm, three in Nazareth, seven in Tel Aviv, two in Beer Sheva, six in Jerusalem and two in Haifa, twenty-three nights in total. Now I must divest myself of the proceeds of my thoughts.

How do the Israelis see themselves?

Years ago, in the mid 1960s to be exact, the famous saying about Israel in the West was that it was the "lighthouse of democracy in the region." These days, after Egypt and several other Arab countries have taken steps towards democracy, a new expression has appeared, first used by Rabin: "We are an island of prosperity in a sea of poverty." This is precisely the source of danger for Israel.

This saying brings to mind what Henry Kissinger said in 1973 when the Arabs announced the oil embargo: "Gazelles should not boast of the quality of their flesh in front of wolves." To be rich in the midst of poverty pushes one to fright and drives peace far away. Thus Shimon Peres said in his interview with the Egyptian newspaper *al-Ahram* on 18 July 1994: "If the standard of living doesn't rise in a large way, we believe the only alternative is the spread of fundamentalism. We want to participate in serious attempts to improve the standard of living and increase the national income and individual incomes among all countries. We don't want to remain an island of luxury amidst a sea of problems."

Note that in the last sentence he used the word "problems," not "poverty," most likely out of politeness. But the saying remains true since poverty will remain forever the greatest source and exporter of problems.

In order to complete the picture, however, let us assume that a creature from a distant planet descends to earth and asks to visit a number of senior Arab officials, journalists and national figures, then asks to visit their Israeli counterparts. Then he returns to his planet. What will he write in his report? He will certainly write: "The Arabs are very rich and the Jews are on the edge of poverty."

I agree with Amos Elon's self-portrait of Israeli society when he wrote: "The Egyptians will be astonished to discover that we are a nation of lower-middle-class people." This is true. They are a disguised middle class. There are no large gaps in income between them. Of course they have poverty, but they strive to lessen its extent and add to the ever-increasing numbers of the broad middle class. History only advances on the shoulders of the middle class, it alone is capable of supplying society with a leading elite in all fields.

On my way south to the Egyptian border, I didn't rely on maps, I just made sure to keep the sun on my right.

What is happening in the region now?

With the end of the Cold War the scope of secrets on earth has narrowed. All the cards of the game are displayed on the table of history. We do not need to steal intelligence documents from the Arabs or the Israelis to know what is happening now. There are Arab countries that have decided one way or another to join the caravan of peace. In my estimation, peace between Syria and Israel will be delayed until the end of the century. The one certainty in the region is that another Arab-Israeli war no longer comes to mind for anyone.

Rising standards of living will define the warmth of the peace. Thus I predict a warm peace between the Arab countries of the Gulf and Israel, which will be warmest between businessmen of the two sides. The region and the entire world will be a stage for their activities.

What about the Palestinians and the Jordanians?

Certainly they will form a single economic unit, dictated by reality and not by slogans. They live on a piece of land meshed together in one neighborhood. The land is stronger and truer than all the minds that walk on it, and it will impose the law of neighborliness on all. The armies of doubt, caution and hatred will be defeated. They will withdraw from the land and the hearts, leaving the way open for the armies of peace, which carry the banners of freedom, education, health, security and justice. Many victims will fall on the way. But this is the destiny of the region.

What about Chairman Arafat and his men?

The only test facing them has one obligatory question: Are you capable of public administrative work?

The mentality of the public administrator is very different from that of the leader. The leader searches for a stirring speech, a surprising political move, or a few vague words that will plant joy in the hearts of the masses. But the public administrator is capable of organizing people, and mobilizing them to work together in a framework of sound legislation and administrative discipline. The public administrator strives for success and accomplishment, while the leader seeks to surprise and paralyze. The public administrator fears the questions of oversight agencies and public opinion, whereas the leader has no oversight except God Almighty. The public administrator records his accounts in notebooks, writes his thoughts in his diary, and keeps his documents in files. The leader keeps the figures of his accounts in his powerful memory, doesn't record his true thoughts in order to protect them from the curious, and doesn't keep files except the ones that incriminate those who work for him.

If anyone imagines that the Palestinians in the West Bank and Gaza can be ruled by a patriarchal totalitarian regime, then he is deluding himself. Fortunately, the delusion will be short-lived, until elections are held. If some people believe they can achieve success by barely passing the obligatory question on the test, then in all likelihood they will successfully "graduate" from the region as former leaders.

The Egyptian border was still distant but I was on the right road, the sun on my right.

Who governs Israel?

I note first for the reader that I do not claim my thoughts are infallibly correct, they correspond imperfectly to the details of reality. I am not a walking center for political research, I am only recording on paper what my mind has comprehended.

The street, the press, mayors and caution govern Israel. As for the central government, it focuses on high politics. Each mayor is responsible for running his city or village. They have made a major discovery: there are a large number of human beings who are good at administrating cities and movements of citizens. Indeed God Almighty, when he bestowed a huge amount of wisdom, patriotism and feelings of responsibility on government ministers and those who work for them, at the same time gave the same amount of these capabilities and talents to others.

I will digress a little here to recall for the reader a story from the Bible (Exodus, chapter 18). This story perhaps has a connection with the formative elements of the Jewish mind and of the Western mind more generally. It is about an incident that happened to Moses and his people after they left Egypt.

"The next day, Moses sat as magistrate among the people, while the people stood about Moses from morning until evening. But when Moses' father-in-law saw how much he had to do for the people, he said, 'What is this thing that you are doing to the people? Why do you act alone, while all the people stand about you from morning until evening?' Moses replied to his father-in-law, 'It is because the people come to me to inquire of God. When they have a dispute, it comes before me, and I decide between one person and another, and I make known the laws and teachings of God.'

"But Moses' father-in-law said to him, 'The thing you are doing is not right; you will surely wear yourself out and these people as well. For the task is too heavy for you; you cannot do it alone. Now listen to me. I will give you counsel, and God be with you! You represent the people before God: You bring the disputes before God, and enjoin upon them the laws and the teachings, and make known to them the way they are to go and the practices they are to follow. You shall also seek out from among all the people capable men who fear God, trustworthy men who spurn ill-gotten gain. Set these over them as chiefs of thousands, hundreds, fifties, and tens, and let them judge the people at all times. Have them bring every major dispute to you, but let them decide every minor dispute themselves. Make it easier for yourself by letting them share the burden with you. If you do this — and God so commands you — you will be able to bear up; and all these people too will go home unwearied.'"[31]

We are facing here the issue of public administration, an issue purely of this world with no role whatsoever for heaven. Even our master Moses, the great prophet and man of miracles, needed to learn the rules of administration from his father-in-law, the tribal sheikh who had long experience in running the affairs of his people. The question is: Wasn't our master Moses aware of these most fundamental principles of governance, having been raised in the palaces of the ruling elite in Pharaonic Egypt and not having left Egypt until he was more than eighty years old?

I say that he knew. Moreover, he knew much more than this about the secrets of governing and administration. It was he who planned and organized the exodus of an entire people in secret. He knew, but knowledge is not sufficient, as they say in psychology. He was a human being after all, and he needed another human being to warn him of a mistake. But why his father-in-law? Why didn't someone from his people come forward to say these words, didn't they direct at him many crude expressions during the exodus journey?

The answer is implicit in the first words, "the next day." They had only arrived the day before, and it was the first day of work, the first political meeting. The Israelites were as yet unclear about the rules by which they would be governed, and they were looking forward to learning them. But there was a long-term danger which Moses' father-in-law perceived and which caused him to intervene at once. Moses' father-in-law was aware that every people feels very comfortable when released of work and responsibility. It is extremely pleasant to sit on the ground without work from morning to evening, enjoying the exposition of one's problems and listening to the problems of others.

Whenever people notice an initiative towards individual rule, they feel great happiness and do not demand good, just administration until individual rule brings them to the gates of Hell. They might even delay this demand until finding themselves between the tongues of the flames and the depths of Hell itself. Some peoples are probably content in the hellfire, since they consider it their inescapable fate, or because the organs of media have convinced them that outside, the cold is fatal.

I approached the Egyptian border.

The Barbed Wire Fence on the Border

In the far south, only a few meters between me and the Egyptian border. I could see the barbed wire fence from here, and behind it a farm covered with green. I was at a place covered with sand, a military area around which were dispersed several kiosks. I sipped coffee and ate some pastries in front of a small kiosk mounted on a trailer. The owner was an Iraqi Jewish woman, and with her a young boy. She insisted on taking only two and a half shekels, the price of the coffee, while the glass of water and the pastries were free of charge since I was an Egyptian guest.

"Keep the barbed wire on your left...after several hundred meters you will find the Rafah Gate."

But before I cross the border into Egypt I have a message to Jews in Israel and throughout the world: Egyptians do not practice racism and you were not slaves to the Egyptian people. I will furnish the evidence for this presently, relying on one source, the Bible, the books of Genesis and Exodus to be precise.

A barbed wire fence has often stood between peoples in the past, causing ancient injuries that did not mend with time, even if we imagined that they did. These injuries hindered the progress of man, even among the great minds. Memories of this hurt expunged from our conscious may slip into the depths of our subconscious and reside there, ready to re-emerge and announce themselves at the moment they deem appropriate.

Among these ancient injuries, one of the most painful is that you were slaves of the Egyptians. But I challenge this common knowledge. The truth to which I adhere, and will explain, is that your troubles in Egypt before the Exodus were with the Egyptian authorities, and they were for political and not racial or religious reasons. Your relations with the Egyptian people were relations of generosity, equality and great affection.

***

In 1990 in America, in a meeting between Jews and Arabs, I asked a question that led to a debate: "Show me evidence of one incident of persecution of Jews in Egypt before 1948."

A Jewish woman looked at me in astonishment and condemnation and said: "The slavery under which we suffered at your hands in ancient Egypt. We were your slaves and built the pyramids by forced labor."

Peres asked the Jews to "put behind them" some incidents of history for the sake of the future, but I know well how difficult this is for the human mind. Thus I have a more modest demand and it is that we have the courage and ability to read with intellectual honesty. The Bible says: "Each woman shall borrow from her neighbor and the lodger in her house objects of silver and gold, and clothing." (Exodus, chapter 3.)

I don't need a big imagination to envision this scene from the depths of history. You were not living on the outskirts of the city or village or in isolated quarters reserved for Jews. You lived with us in the same quarters. You were our neighbors, in fact living in the same houses. The relations between us permitted the Jewish woman to ask the Egyptian woman for objects of silver and gold and clothing, and they were given.

When in the course of history did a slave have the courage to ask things of this sort from his master? According to an ancient Egyptian custom, present in the countryside to this day, a peasant woman asks her neighbor for jewelry and expensive clothing to wear in a wedding party or other joyous occasion, then returns them on the morning of the following day. When we agree that you were slaves in Egypt at that time, then we must record that Egyptians were also slaves like you and with you.

We must also beware of the trap of using the same concept for different periods of history. Was slavery in Egypt as mentioned in the Torah the same as bondage as we know it from much more recent days in Europe and America? I don't have a definitive answer, but we should together think of a reasonable answer as we review what happened.

Our master Joseph came to Egypt and was bought by Potiphar, the chief of the guards, a position we would perhaps call in today's parlance the "director of public security." Owing to our master Joseph's moral honesty, administrative competence and trustworthiness, Potiphar left him to administer both his private and public affairs. Please note that as an Egyptian Arab Muslim, I don't say the name "Joseph" alone, but add "our master Joseph." For the sake of simplicity of recital, however, permit me to use his proper name alone after I have confirmed that he is a master to me. Later Joseph was exposed to the painful experience with the man's wife, when she accused him of assault and attempted rape. So they put him in prison, not in any prison but a special prison for those out of favor in the Pharaoh's palace. This is an ancient Egyptian custom still in use. When members of the regime or those close to them are imprisoned for one reason or another, they are put in a special place inside the general prison.

It is strange that the prison warden also left Joseph to administer the prison despite the fact that he was one of its residents. We note that Joseph was not exposed to physical punishment of any type, or the Bible would have so stated. I surmise that Potiphar, the security official who had previously handled dozens of liars, murderers and criminals, was certain that his wife had lied, that her story was invented, and that Joseph was innocent. But he had to put Joseph in prison. The only alternative was to punish the wife herself, which would have resulted in a scandal with consequences for a man of his weighty position. So he turned Joseph over to the prison warden, one of his subordinates, who knew all the circumstances, and knew that Joseph was competent and wronged. Later we find Joseph assuming the administration of all of Egypt, the chief vizier and deputy to the Pharaoh, after being given the Pharaoh's seal with the authority to take any decision he wanted.

Was Joseph the foreign Jewish slave appointed to this position only for his extraordinary ability to interpret dreams? It is a good thing, indeed a miracle, for a man to interpret the dreams of the slender and fat cows and the ears of grain. But did this decide the matter of his appointment to this position? Would the circles of power inside the palace, the priests and others, have permitted this? Or did the appointment come as a result of his past, his administrative talent, and intellectual and moral honesty which was well known to the ruling classes? They later married him to a daughter of the priest of On as a natural matter.

I don't believe any culture in history surpassed the ancient Egyptians in believing in the importance of moral and intellectual honesty and administrative talent. No one stood in the palace shouting or whispering in the Pharaoh's ear: "But he is a Jew, my Lord."

Yet such a sentence was spoken, with racist disdain.

Who said this, and in what circumstances? We will know this shortly, after reading Genesis, chapter 39:

"After a time, his master's wife cast her eyes upon Joseph and said, 'Lie with me.' But he refused and said to his master's wife, 'Look, with me here, my master gives no thought to anything in this house, and all that he owns he has placed in my hands. He wields no more authority in this house than I, and he has withheld nothing from me except yourself, since you are his wife. How then could I do this most wicked thing, and sin before God?' And much as she coaxed Joseph day after day, he did not yield to her request to lie beside her, to be with her.

"One such day, he came into the house to do his work. None of the household being there inside, she caught hold of him by his garment and said, 'Lie with me!' But he left his garment in her hand and got away and fled outside. When she saw that he had left it in her hand and had fled outside, she called out to her servants and said to them, 'Look, he had to bring us a Hebrew to dally with us! This one came to lie with me; but I screamed loud. And when he heard me screaming at the top of my voice, he left his garment with me and got away and fled outside.'"

I will pause at one sentence: "Look, he had to bring us a Hebrew to dally with us." Only Potiphar's wife talks in this racist way. As for the palace, wherein resides responsibility and intellectual maturity, no one says: "Should we appoint this Hebrew or this Jewish slave to this weighty position?" It didn't happen for a simple reason. Egyptians didn't practice racism.

Joseph was engrossed in his hard work of gathering grain and storing it to confront the coming famine. His brothers came to Egypt asking for grain. The famine included the entire region. Then they came a second time and he invited them to the palace to share a meal. In the palace he asked them: "How is your aged father of whom you spoke? Is he still in good health?" They replied, "It is well with your servant our father; he is still in good health." And they bowed and made obeisance.

"He gave the order, 'Serve the meal.' They served him by himself, and them by themselves, and the Egyptians who ate with him by themselves; for the Egyptians could not dine with the Hebrews, since that would be abhorrent to the Egyptians." (Genesis, chapter 43.)

Of course my desire to defend the ancient Egyptians doesn't preclude me from acknowledging the possibility of their possessing racist beliefs or behavior. We must take into consideration that this ancient valley, the Nile Valley, has passed through long periods of cultural efflorescence and other periods of decline. In the periods of decline it is very possible that racist ideas spread over the years, and especially in a climate controlled by the "media of hatred." There is certainly no end to the mire in which the human mind can sink when it is stricken with decline. I know a man of influence in the present age and in this area who spreads the rumor through powerful media means that merely shaking the hands of people of other religions is blasphemy.[32]

But I cannot resist the temptation to shed light on this scene from the viewpoint of an Egyptian dramatist. It deals with an incident replete with dramatic elements and with Egyptian customs, tradition and behavior.

Joseph invited his brothers to share a meal in his great palace, the palace of the deputy to the Pharaoh. He has not yet informed them that he is their brother. In the palace he feels a strong desire to cry, these are his brothers who had wanted to kill him. He shuts himself in one of the rooms of the palace, cries, gets control of himself, goes out to greet them in the great dining hall and orders the meal to be served. He eats by himself, the Egyptians by themselves and the Hebrews by themselves, but not because Egyptians abhor sharing a meal with Jews.

It is a scene well known in the popular literature of all ancient cultures. With a sign from the highest authority the servants begin putting down food and drink. The routine would be familiar to the servants of the palace. Joseph finishes his work every day at a fixed time and returns with his guests or they precede him to the palace. Every day at this time there are Egyptian and foreign guests. If we assume that Egyptians abhor sharing a meal with Hebrews and thus they are served separately, why didn't Joseph share his meal with the Hebrew guests? All the Egyptians and the workers in the palace know that he is a Hebrew. Of course no one at this moment knew that these strange shepherds were Joseph's brothers, but certainly all Egypt knew that he was a Hebrew.

We can try another assumption, that the highest ranks of authority in Egypt represented by Joseph made the Egyptians forget or pretend to forget his Hebrew origin. They consider him, just as he considers himself, an Egyptian. Then why didn't he share his meal with the Egyptians? Why did he eat alone?

It is an ancient Egyptian custom still practiced today. When the social levels differ sharply, those of the lowest level will not feel comfortable sharing a meal with the higher level. Thus one must out of hospitality give the lower level the opportunity to eat "at his comfort" as we say in Egypt. The act of eating a meal in Egypt has its peculiarities, in fact traditionally there were people who considered food a private bodily matter and no one should see you while you are eating.

I noticed once that the playwright Bahig Ismail, when we went out together with a group of friends and ordered dinner, stood up and went to eat at a distant table. When I asked him for the reason he said: "The sight of people eating is not pleasant to behold." In short, he removed himself to eat at his comfort. Until very recently, as depicted in Naguib Mahfouz's novel *Midaq Alley*, the head of the household would have dinner placed before him by himself, so that he could eat far from the children and people of the house at his comfort.

Joseph's brothers were a group of shepherds coming from the interior of the desert. A short while ago they had bowed and paid him obeisance. Would they feel comfortable eating a meal at the same table with the occupant of the highest position in Egypt? The matter is not that they are Hebrews, in that he also did not sit at the table with his Egyptian guests, and they were certainly senior officials of the state.

***

Using the vocabulary of the age, I say to you: Thousands of years ago, you came to Egypt by invitation of the Egyptian government, sponsored by it and using Egyptian means of transportation, with the guarantees of comfort, sustenance and security on the road, then provision of residence, land and welfare.

"The news reached Pharaoh's palace: Joseph's brothers have come. Pharaoh and his courtiers were pleased. And Pharaoh said to Joseph, 'Say to your brothers, Do as follows: load up your beasts and go at once to the land of Canaan. Take your father and your households and come to me. I will give you the best of the land of Egypt and you shall live off the fat of the land. And you are bidden to add, Do as follows: Take from the land of Egypt wagons for your children and your wives, and bring your father here. And never mind your belongings, for the best of all the land of Egypt shall be yours.'" (Genesis, chapter 45.)

I don't believe another king in history made this kind of generous offer to a group of foreigners, but I understand it naturally in light of the glorious services that Joseph performed for the state. He deserved all that the Pharaoh ordered for him and his family in appreciation of his role in managing the drought crisis in Egypt.

Our master Jacob came to Egypt and you came with him. All that Pharaoh promised to you was realized, the treasures of Egypt and the fat of the land. And when Jacob died in Egypt, he was embalmed according to Egyptian custom for forty days and a period of seventy days of public mourning was announced. Then a large Egyptian caravan accompanied him to his burial in the land of Canaan in accordance with his request.

"Chariots and horsemen went up with him; it was a very large troop. When they came to Goren ha-Atad, which is beyond the Jordan, they held there a very great and solemn lamentation; and he observed a mourning period of seven days for his father. And when the Canaanite inhabitants of the land saw the mourning at Goren ha-Atad, they said, 'This is a solemn mourning on the part of the Egyptians.' That is why the place was named 'Avel Mitsrayim,' the mourning of Egypt." (Genesis, chapter 50.)

Who accompanied the body of Jacob? All of the officials and public figures of Egypt. That is the answer in the Bible.

Returning To Egypt

Then came the time when you were slaves to Pharaoh, and we also were slaves to him with you. We must keep in mind the possibility that slavery meant something different at that time. You were treated badly before the Exodus, on this I strongly agree. But we must understand what happened from a political viewpoint and in light of the mechanisms of history, not to justify but rather to interpret it, in my view, as a natural and in fact inevitable occurrence.

Egypt prepared for the drought. Joseph managed the crisis with high political skill and great effort. He drew up a plan for storing grain throughout the land then supervised its implementation. In times of plenty, people hated to merely think that hunger is on its way. The drought occurred, and Egyptians came and obtained grain after they paid its price. They continued to pay for what they needed until their liquidity was finished. They were bankrupt, they had nothing left to pay. Would Joseph give them grain for free?

An exchange of goods was required, otherwise, the entire economy in Egypt would have collapsed. The people were hungry in the end. Certainly some would obtain the shares of the other people, as usually occurs in political systems which partly or totally subsidize goods. The Egyptians gave what they owned, animals and livestock in exchange for grain. But the digestive system of human beings required that people must continue to eat. Once again, the Egyptians were hungry. What to do?

They gave their land and their bodies in exchange for food. From that moment the entire land of Egypt and what was on it, including animals and human beings, became the property of Pharaoh.

"Now there was no bread in all the world, for the famine was very severe; both the land of Egypt and the land of Canaan languished because of the famine. Joseph gathered in all the money that was to be found in the land of Egypt and in the land of Canaan, as payment for the rations that were being procured, and Joseph brought the money into the Pharaoh's palace. And when the money gave out in the land of Egypt and in the land of Canaan, all the Egyptians came to Joseph and said, 'Give us bread, lest we die before your very eyes; for the money is gone.' And Joseph said, 'Bring your livestock, and I will sell to you against your livestock, if the money is gone.' So they brought their livestock to Joseph, and

Joseph gave them bread in exchange for the horses, for the stocks of sheep and cattle, and the asses; thus he provided them with bread that year in exchange for all their livestock. And when that year was ended, they came to him the next year and said to him, 'We cannot hide from my lord that, with all the money and animal stocks consigned to my lord, nothing is left at my lord's disposal save our persons and our farmland. Let us not perish before your eyes, both we and our land. Take us and our land in exchange for bread, and we with our land will be serfs to Pharaoh; provide the seed, that we may live and not die, and that the land may not become a waste.'

"So Joseph gained possession of all the farm land of Egypt for Pharaoh, every Egyptian having sold his field because the famine was too much for them; thus the land passed over to Pharaoh. And he removed the population town by town, from one end of Egypt's border to the other. Only the land of the priests he did not take over, for the priests had an allotment from Pharaoh, and they lived off the allotment which Pharaoh had made to them; therefore they did not sell their land.

"Then Joseph said to the people, 'Whereas I have this day acquired you and your land for Pharaoh, here is seed for you to sow the land. And when harvest comes, you shall give one-fifth to Pharaoh, and four-fifths shall be yours as seed for the fields and as food for you and those in your households, and as nourishment for your children.' And they said, 'You have saved our lives! We are grateful to my lord, and we shall be serfs to Pharaoh.' And Joseph made it into a land law in Egypt, which is still valid, that a fifth should be Pharaoh's; only the land of the priests did not become Pharaoh's." (Genesis, chapter 47.)

This is the picture then, a regime that owns the land and all that is on it. One must recognize that a fifth of the harvest is a very reasonable tax in comparison with today. But one must also recognize that the loss of private property leaves bitterness in the throat and a rancor in the heart that the passing of days does not erase.

It is clear also that a number of people were resettled. "And he removed the population town by town, from one end of Egypt's border to the other." This benefited the public good, of course, but only philosophers and statesmen understand the expression "the public good." The peasants only complain, but they carry out the task in the end because they are not free.

***

Joseph the powerful statesman died. Hundreds of years went by and a crisis emerged with change in the political system. Another Pharaoh came from another family. "A new king arose over Egypt who did not know Joseph. And he said to his people, 'Look, the Israelite people are much too numerous for us. Let us deal shrewdly with them, so that they may not increase, otherwise in the event of war they may join our enemies in fighting against us and rise from the ground.'" (Exodus, chapter 1.)

One of the stable traditions of rule in the Middle East generally and the Nile Valley in particular is that a new dynasty wipes out all traces of the prior dynasty. It destroys all the remaining pillars of its predecessor, and is focused for many years on purifying the country of the "corruption" of the prior regime, to which it gives the name "the bygone age." We have Pharaohs who made do with wiping out the name of the prior king from the prior king's monuments, and inserting their own names. I feel a certain amount of respect for these Pharaohs; they were content with stealing work rather than destroying it. If the issue is connected with "regime protection" in case of war, or the threat or suspicion of war, then measures to protect the regime require first of all to confine the minority and restrict it as probable aides to the enemy. In the modern lexicon they are called fifth columnists, counter-revolutionary elements, aides or tails of colonialism, or agents of international imperialism, etc.

"A new king arose over Egypt." This king did not arrive on the throne in a calm or natural way, through inheritance for example, but he "arose" over Egypt. We use the word "arose" to describe a sudden occurrence characterized by violence: a war arose, a revolution arose, his world arose and did not return. It was an upheaval then in the regime, an interpretation strengthened by the word "new." He had no connection to what preceded him and was not an extension of it. He was a new king who arose over Egypt and its people. And he "did not know" Joseph, meaning that he did not recognize Joseph or Joseph's glorious service to the state, for a simple reason. Joseph and all his people belonged to the "bygone age" and its pillars must be torn down. This is the rule.

It is of course easy to imagine the organs of a powerful media at work in the palace, the temples of the priests and councils of the officials, churning out stories of aggression and hatred, fear of the coming war and the likelihood of Hebrew cooperation with the enemy. Then as a result came the bad treatment ending with the Exodus from Egypt. As for the common Egyptian people, they were connected to you with ties of friendship, as witnessed by the incident of your asking for their gold, silver and clothes.

Isn't this exactly what happened in the first half of the twentieth century in the strongest modern civilization? In America, directly after the attack on Pearl Harbor, violent and abusive measures were taken against Americans of Japanese origin out of fear of their collaboration with the enemy. Japanese Americans were only able to obtain compensation through a decision of the Supreme Court more than forty years later.

But the words spoken by the new Pharaoh do not indicate racism or denigration. There were no bad words about the Hebrews of the sort so common in European political speech for centuries. He used, in the final analysis, the vocabulary of political science, without any hint of the insult of racism.

***

Standing on the corner of the last street of the twentieth century, and glancing at the insane massacres that have occurred and will occur in Europe, Africa and the Middle East, I wish I could return back thousands of years, to enjoy life in Egypt when it was more civilized, tolerant and glorious.

Perhaps the reader in Egypt is surprised at my interest in a historical incident so ancient that its effects seem to have vanished from human minds. But I say to them: I am replying at length, through my reading of the Bible, to the woman who accused me in America, and to the thousands who believe what she believes. For them, the ancient moment lives next to or rather inside of the present moment. The Egyptian Jewish diplomat who said to me, "we went out from Egypt twice," placed the two moments side by side and on equal footing. He left Egypt as a small child but he still feels the pain of going out twice, because he summoned from his memory the Exodus and attached it to the present moment and so doubled his pain.

If it is impossible to change the events of history, then it is always possible to understand them better, in light of human nature and for the sake of guiding man's path toward the final destination, which is one family of mankind. We are not permitted to rewrite history. But man's honor and his interests as well dictate that he write the blank pages, the ones that haven't yet been written. And when we write them, we must cease working as slaves to History. We must prevent History from pursuing its ancient loathsome habit of acting as a butcher in its free time.

We must immediately cease working as slaves to History. It is History that should work for us, it should carry out our desires. We should say to it "thus" and it will be so.

**

I must not get too close to the barbed wire border fence so that its teeth don't sink into my flesh as has happened throughout history to those with good intentions.

I started the motor and took off toward the border fence. I turned right, driving on an unpaved road, the barbed wire of the border on my left. Over the border, two soldiers were standing on a watchtower. I pressed on the gas pedal and honked the horn. The two soldiers saw the Egyptian license plate and began shouting and cheering. I didn't stop, I waved to them and rushed towards the border crossing at top speed, honking the horn. I didn't use it during the entire trip, why now? And why did the two soldiers cheer? Why did a tear flow from my eye?

I don't know.

I finished the Israeli customs and passport procedures and calmly approached the Egyptian border gate. A police lieutenant and two corporals stood up and looked at me and my car in amazement. The lieutenant took my passport, threw me a glance then said: "Yes, mister?"

A moment of terror passed over me. My confidence in the Egyptian bureaucracy is non-existent. Is it possible that in my absence they issued a decree not allowing Egyptians to return from abroad? I said to him, attempting to sound natural: "What is it, my son? This is an Egyptian car...and I am an Egyptian returning to Egypt."

Moments passed as if they were a lifetime. He called his chief who gave permission for me to enter. I thought of my words; was I really returning to Egypt?

By God, I never left her and she will never leave me for one moment.

Ali Salem
Cairo, August 1994

NOTES

1. The equivalent of about $5,000 at the time.
2. An Egyptian meal of boiled and fried broad beans.
3. Umm al-Fahm is a town of about 36,000 Arab citizens of Israel located in the Western Galilee.
4. *Shawarma* is a dish of thinly sliced pieces of roasted lamb cut from a rotisserie.
5. On 25 February 1994, an Israeli settler in Hebron opened fire on Muslim worshippers in the Tomb of the Patriarchs, killing twenty-nine persons.
6. Damietta, like Jaffa, is a Mediterranean port city. Damietta lies at the mouth of the eastern branch of the Nile.
7. According to Egyptian custom, when a family member dies the family sets up a tent of mourning on the evening of the funeral and stays in it to receive calls of condolence.
8. This is the pitcher of water used by Muslims to wash their face, hands, arms and feet before prayer.
9. *Yediot Aharonot* is a popular Hebrew-language daily newspaper.
10. An Israeli labor union organization.
11. *School of the Troublemakers* is Salem's most popular play. An Egyptian version of *To Sir With Love*, it was adapted into a film shown throughout the Arab world and starred Egypt's leading comedic actor Adel Imam.
12. Habibi was drawing on the lyrics of a song by Egyptian composer Sayyid Darwish, "Visit me Once a Year," popularized by the Lebanese chanteuse Feiruz.
13. A quote from "Majnoun Laila," the epic poem of Egypt's "prince of poets" Ahmad Shawqi. It is the tale of the tragic love affair between the pre-Islamic Arabian hero Qais and Laila, the daughter of a sheikh from another tribe.
14. A school of early Muslim theologians known for their rationalism.
15. A reference to the 1994 civil war in Yemen.
16. The province that includes Egypt's western desert oases.
17. Hasan al-Banna founded the Muslim Brotherhood, a fundamentalist political group. Ahmad Hussein founded Young Egypt, an extreme nationalist group. Fathy Radwan was a founder of the Nationalist Party, which broke off from Young Egypt. Abdallah Lamloum, a wealthy landowner from rural al-Minya province, was a member of the moderate nationalist Saadist group.
18. The names Abdullah and Ovadiah both mean "servant of God" in Arabic and Hebrew respectively.
19. A reference to an incident in 1974, when Rabin had returned from his post as Israel's ambassador to the U.S. but maintained an American bank account. At the time, Israelis were not allowed to maintain bank accounts abroad.
20. A reference to Syrian poet Nizar Qabbani's poem "The Scurrying Ones."
21. Naguib Mahfouz, Egypt's Nobel prize laureate for literature; the late Taha Hussein, famed Egyptian novelist and critic; Ahmad Bahaeddin, one of Egypt's

leading journalists and commentators; al-Mutannabi, tenth-century poet from Iraq; al-Jahiz, ninth-century prose writer from Iraq; and the "Eloquent Peasant," the hero of an ancient Egyptian parable.

22. Al-Sunbati, al-Qassabgi, Abdel Wahhab, and Baligh Hamdi are all modern Egyptian composers.

23. Mitsrayim is the Hebrew word for Egypt.

24. The Cairo Agreement, also called the Gaza-Jericho Agreement, was signed on 4 May 1994 by Israel and the PLO. It implemented Palestinian self-rule in the Gaza Strip and the West Bank city of Jericho.

25. The Aragoz is a famous clown character in the national theater of Egypt.

26. Umm Kulthoum is Egypt's most famous female singer and Muhammad Abdel Wahhab is Egypt's most famous modern composer.

27. *Davar* was at the time the Israeli Labor Party's organ.

28. After implementation of their 1979 peace agreement, Egypt and Israel entered into arbitration over a small parcel of land in Sinai called Taba. The arbitration was resolved in Egypt's favor in 1989.

29. The Arabic word for "axe," *fa's*, is taken from the Latin word, *fasces*, the Roman symbol of sovereignty.

30. Salem lost a brother in the 1973 Arab-Israeli war.

31. The English translation of the Bible quoted here and in following chapters is taken from Holy Scriptures, Jewish Publication Society, 1985.

32. A reference to an Egyptian fundamentalist preacher popular in the early 1990's, Umar Abdel Kafi', who used to exhort his congregants in the wealthy Cairo neighborhood of Dokki not to shake hands with non-Muslims.